Beef and Liberty

For Pam
who believes in both
with love
Savas and Girish
19.05.03

By the same author

Pascal: In Praise of Vanity
A.J. Ayer: A Life

Beef and Liberty

Ben Rogers

Chatto & Windus
LONDON

Published by Chatto & Windus 2003

2 4 6 8 10 9 7 5 3 1

First published in Great Britain in 2003 by
Chatto & Windus
Random House, 20 Vauxhall Bridge Road,
London SW1V 2SA

Random House Australia (Pty) Limited
20 Alfred Street, Milsons Point, Sydney,
New South Wales 2061, Australia

Random House New Zealand Limited
18 Poland Road, Glenfield,
Auckland 10, New Zealand

Random House (Pty) Limited
Endulini, 5A Jubilee Road, Parktown 2193, South Africa

The Random House Group Limited Reg. No. 954009
www.randomhouse.co.uk

A CIP catalogue record for this book is available from the British Library

ISBN 0 7011 6980 X

Papers used by Random House are natural, recyclable products made from wood grown in sustainable forests; the manufacturing processes conform to the environmental regulations of the country of origin.

Typeset by SX Composing DTP, Rayleigh, Essex
Printed and bound in Great Britain by Biddles Ltd, Guildford and King's Lynn.

For Harriet

Contents

List of Illustrations

Should the French dare invade us, thus armed with our poles,
We'll bang their bare ribs, make their lantern jaws ring:
For you beef-eating, beer-drinking Britons are souls
Who will shed their last blood for their country and king.

Drinking song, *c.*1757

Englishmen are patriots with their whole body, not only in their heart; their stomach also seems here to feel for the native land. And I have often seen Englishmen round their dinner-table, busy with their roast beef in as quiet and proud a felicity as if they felt the whole worth of their favoured island on their tongues.

Geijer, *Impressions of England, 1809–10*

Wool and flesh are the primitive foundations of England and the English race . . . From time immemorial they were a breeding and pastoral people – a race fatted on beef and mutton. Hence that freshness of tint, that beauty and strength. Their greatest man, Shakespeare, was originally a butcher.

Jules Michelet, *History of France*, 1843

Sir, Earlier this year, my wife and I travelled across France en route to Austria. At our overnight hotel in Metz, we had what must hold first place in any list of disastrous meals.

The main course was 'roast beef'. French beef, of course. It was tough, it was dry, it was flavourless. It was undoubtedly the worst beef I have ever tasted, and was accompanied by four sauté potatoes that were obviously the leftover boiled potatoes from lunch. The beef was so awful that we wondered if in fact it had come from the sole of the chef's boot.

How dare they criticise our beef, when they expect us to consume meat from animals that have been fed on sewage?

Letter to the *Daily Telegraph*, 28 October 1999

Introduction

Sir, Could you follow up Hogarth's picture today (Anniversaries), with *The Gate of Calais* in which, in 1748, he showed the triumphant entry of English Beef into France?

He remains topical.

Letter to *The Times*, 28 October 1999

THIS BOOK IS a result of mad cow disease. More accurately, it has its origins in the humiliating blow that BSE (bovine spongiform encephalopathy) seemed to deal to British national pride. During the mid-1990s, following the establishment of a link between the disease and the appearance of a new and fatal condition afflicting growing numbers of Britons, variant CJD, Britain's beef exports collapsed. Even after a 1998 European Community ruling that British beef was safe, France, hitherto a major importer of British beef, refused to lift its ban. These developments provoked both shame and anger. English farmers marched on the Houses of Parliament with pigs and cows, one even coming dressed as John Bull. English shops and shoppers started an unofficial boycott of French goods. French vendors were advised not to set up their street-market stalls in England for fear that they would be attacked. Patriotic newspapers offered up tit-for-tat stories about the muck fed to French cows and the cruel conditions in which the French kept their pigs. I was vaguely aware, as most of us were, that beef and associated symbols of John Bull and the bulldog had long been identified with England, and I appreciated that only this could explain why sections of the British population reacted to the French ban in the way they did. I decided to find out more.

My investigations took me back to the seventeenth and eighteenth centuries, for it was during these periods that roast beef, the bulldog and John Bull were first taken up by patriots as emblems of manly English virtues. It was during the eighteenth century, in particular, that 'Beef and Liberty' became a rallying cry for Britons worried about the military threat from France abroad, and from the spread of Gallic luxury and corruption at home. But again and again, while writing this history, I have been struck by how much of it lives on in modern British tastes and attitudes – in, say, the widespread suspicion of Europe, attachment to the countryside and its ways, appetite for blood sports, and a national fondness for meaty, fiery food. Watching television, reading newspapers or walking in the street, I have often heard voices and seen sights from the past. I hope the reader will come to hear and see them, too.

All cultural identity is closely bound up with food and cooking. No one makes an apple pie as good as mother's. The obvious analogy here is with language. Our culinary likes and dislikes, like our mother tongue, feel natural, yet we acquire both through a slow process of youthful acculturation. Taste, like language, changes from family to family, class to class, sect to sect, region to region. There is one respect, in fact, in which our taste for food penetrates us more deeply than language ever can. After a time, tastes acquired in childhood take on an almost visceral quality. A Hindu might find the odour of roast beef positively stomach turning, but a hungry English beef eater will judge it the best smell in the world. Foreign languages can sound funny or barbarous, but foreign food is often physically repellent.

If food helps to mark out all social distinctions, it is particularly important to national ones. It is no exaggeration to say that, after language, food is the most important bearer of national identity. This is particularly true of meat, which is, as anthropologists remind us, the most prized of foods and the one most deeply invested with metaphor.[1] Blood, after all, is the essence of meat, and blood has rich symbolic power. It is the seat of the soul, the root of sexual and violent passions, the special unifying character of race and nation. What better symbolises the 'the blood and soil' of the nation than a bloody slice of beef from a cow fed on grass?

In the modern world national traditions of cookery, especially meat cookery, weave together two strongly valued realms of life. They represent the nation, in the sense that they are enjoyed by compatriots everywhere (and ideally, as in Sunday lunch or Christmas dinner, at the same time). But they also symbolise the hearth and home – national dishes are, at least in theory, lovingly prepared by the mother in her kitchen and enjoyed by the family together. National culinary tradition, in other words, binds happy families into larger national wholes.

It is hardly surprising then that culinary nationalism has always been an important component of a broader nationalism. It was not just British patriots who, in the early days of the nation state, set out to defend native cooking against the alien, impersonal and artificial cooking of France. Their Italian, German, Russian and American counterparts did the same. Similarly, today there is only one thing that bothers French and Italian patriots more than the developing hegemony of the English language and the popularity of American pop culture and that is the erosion of their culinary traditions and the spread of alien, impersonal and artificial 'fast food'. Hence Italian attempts to lay down 'pizza' and 'Parma ham' standards, and French attachment to local sausages and valley cheeses. Hence the slogan of the Italian 'Slow Food' movement – 'Better a bowl of tortellini than a hundred hamburgers' – and the dismantling of a French McDonald's in protest at an American embargo on Roquefort cheese. Even Britain, which is today hardly defined by its cooking, harbours residual traces of this sort of pride in national culinary tradition – and not just in the form of wounded pride at the banning of British beef. Local cheese producers, organic farmers, and farmers' markets have managed to secure a small but growing trade with shoppers who like their food to taste of their native land rather than the factory farm or the supermarket. Pubs still advertise 'traditional roast Sunday lunch' and Prince Charles has launched his own line of 'traditional' hams, bacon and bangers. More imaginatively, a small band of chefs and cookery writers, like Hugh Fearnley-Whittingstall and Fergus Henderson, defying our apparently tireless appetite for factory-produced, microwave-ready pizzas, beef fried rice and chicken enchiladas, have won acclaim for a distinctive style of modern, native English cooking – what might be called 'a cooking of resistance'.[2]

Even in Britain our seemingly boundless appetite for supermarket grub and 'ethnic restaurants' testifies, in an unexpected way, to our appetite for cooking with a sense of place. Within half a mile of where I live in north London, restaurants offer French, Italian, Greek, Portuguese, Thai, Vietnamese, Chinese, Japanese, Indian, Belgian, Swedish and 'traditional' English food – and that is just the beginning. Admittedly, most of these restaurants opened in the last decade and so might well be taken as testimony to the 'globalisation' of modern culture, but that would be too quick. After all, each offers a distinctively national cuisine, while none of the other shops in the neighbourhood – clothes shops, florists, bookshops, toyshops, video stores – confine themselves to goods from one country. Similarly the ready cooked meals offered in the supermarket down the road pay homage to national traditions – although not British ones – in serving 'Chinese sweet and sour ribs', 'Indian chicken tikka' and 'Italian cannelloni'. It seems that we want our food to be grounded in a national tradition, to speak to us of a history and a culture, a terrain and a climate.

As far as I can tell, however, historians and sociologists have not taken much interest in nationalism of the culinary kind. Perhaps the (mainly male) academics who study nationalism think food is trivial

Dave Gaskell cartoon, the *Sun*, 28 October 1998

or frivolous, but they virtually never identify it for what it is – a vitally important ingredient in national identity and a potent source of xenophobia.

I

Beef Eaters

Beef is a good meate for an Englyssheman.

Andrew Boorde, *Compendyous Regyment, or a Dyetary of Health*, 1542

IF YOU HAD wandered on to the ribbon of open field between the woods of Agincourt and Tramecourt in northern France on the night of 24 October 1415, you would have quickly been alerted to unusual goings-on. At one end of the field, a French army of some thirty thousand men was confidently preparing for battle, sharpening weapons, unfurling banners, singing songs around large camp fires. At the other end, half a mile away, a much smaller force of English soldiers, having confessed to their priests, were sheltering from the rain in makeshift tents. It was the end of a long season of military campaigning; they were tired and hungry.

If you crept up to the French commanders, gathered in the midst of their troops, you might have caught snatches of conversation as they waited nervously for the sun to rise. Had you got even closer, you could have heard them begin to deride the 'peevish' English king and his 'fat-brained' followers. You might also have heard one of the French lords interjecting a note of caution:

LORD RAMBURES: That Island of England breeds very valiant creatures: their mastiffs are of unmatchable courage . . .

CONSTABLE OF FRANCE: Just, just; and the men do sympathise with the mastiffs in robustious and rough coming on, leaving their wits with their wives; and then, give them great meals of beef . . . they will eat like wolves and fight like devils.

DUKE OF ORLEANS: Ay, but these English are shrewdly out of beef.

CONSTABLE OF FRANCE: Then shall we find tomorrow they have only stomachs to eat, and none to fight. Now is it time to arm. Come, shall we about it?

DUKE OF ORLEANS:

It is now two o'clock: but, let me see – by ten
   We shall have each a hundred Englishmen.

Early the next day both the French forces and the English, commanded by the young Henry V, formed themselves into three lines. But where the great mass of the French army was made up of 'men-at-arms', gentlemen mounted on horses and clad in old-fashioned, heavy armour, the smaller English force was divided between dismounted knights and lightly armoured yeomen wielding short swords and longbows. For three hours after sunrise the two armies stood facing each other. Then the English advanced. The archers fixed pointed stakes into the ground to ward off enemy cavalry and opened the engagement with flights of arrows. The French were at last stung into action and charged. Hemmed in by woods on both sides and the cavalry behind, and hampered by their armour, they began to fall over one another in confusion. Those who were not felled by English arrows or slain by English swords, suffocated in a mash of mud and tangled armour.

The second line of the French now came forward, but they too were killed or taken. Most of the men of the third line fled. Henry V and his high-tech, versatile yeoman archers had won the day, and the

Battle of Agincourt would rank with Crécy and Poitiers, Blenheim and Trafalgar in the roll call of England's great victories over France. Like other nations, England was very largely formed out of the experience of shared triumphs and travails. Agincourt was an important milestone.

All right, if you *had* found yourself hemmed in by those woods on that night, you would *not* have heard that conversation, or one remotely like it. The words are Shakespeare's, from *Henry V*, Act III, Scene 7, written in 1599, nearly two hundred years after the event. It is nonetheless telling that Shakespeare chose to put those words into the mouths of Frenchmen on the eve of one of England's greatest military victories – and in his most patriotic play. For while England did not become indelibly associated with beef, bulls and bulldogs until the eighteenth century, *Henry V* suggests that the association had a history. Shakespeare's lines show that the English already saw themselves as a bullish, mastiff-owning, beef-eating people by the end of the 1590s and that this was connected, in their minds, with their valour.

It is strangely hard to trace the early stages of the emergence of roast beef as a patriotic emblem. The association seems to have begun as a network of subterranean streams that occasionally emerge into the light of day, and then suddenly burst forth as a sizeable river late in the seventeenth century. Nevertheless, a few key points seem certain.

First, by the time Shakespeare was writing, the English were, relatively speaking, great meat eaters. As elsewhere, the type and quantity of meat eaten varied from class to class, place to place and season to season. If at the top of the pile, the gentry feasted on little but flesh, those living near the bottom – a cottager, say, or an unskilled urban labourer – hardly ever tasted it, getting by instead on a diet of gruel, bread, pulses, onions and cabbages, supplemented during good times by cheese and eggs – 'white meate' – or the odd wild fish or fowl. If he was a little richer, a smallholder or artisan might keep chickens, a pig, or perhaps a cow. Pigs were especially easy to rear, as they could be fed on scraps and refuse and their meat lasted well when cured, so that bacon had long been the poor man's meat.

Even between these extremes, there were notable variations. To the husbandman who cultivated a couple of acres of corn or the small tenant farmer who kept a few scrawny animals on the common, meat was still a comparative rarity – and when he ate it, it was as often as not in its salted form. The rich yeoman, by contrast, who grazed several hundred head of livestock on his newly enclosed fields, the successful city merchant, or the wealthy squire who rented out large tracts of farmland, could expect to eat meat every day.[1]

However varied the picture, the evidence suggests that the English ate, on average, more meat than their neighbours. England developed market institutions and reliable food supplies early on, so that by the Tudor period the country was wealthier than most of its neighbours and its wealth was spread relatively widely. (After rising through most of the 1500s, labourers' wages did fall dramatically in the course of the sixteenth and seventeenth centuries; but the 'middling rank' of substantial husbandmen, yeomen and gentlemen, craftsmen, traders and professionals grew significantly richer.) It would have been strange if this prosperity had not led to the middle and upper classes eating comparatively large quantities of meat. In fact the price of beef and mutton declined through the sixteenth and seventeenth centuries in relation to most things including other basic foods. This was a period of considerable inflation, but where the price of rye increased eight times from 1500 to 1650, wheat seven times, peas six and eggs and milk four, that of beef only doubled.[2]

Sixteenth- and seventeenth-century English travellers frequently complained about the expense and poor quality of meat abroad. In the

1570s, the English traveller Sir Richard Morison recorded that 'Venice is as big, or very little less, than London with the suburbs: yet there is more flesh spent in two or three months in London than is there in a year'.[3] More significantly, given that Englishmen were naturally biased in their country's favour, foreign travellers often commented on the easy availability of meat in England.

An Italian merchant, Alessandro Magno, who visited London in 1562, four years into Elizabeth's reign, was astonished at the amount of flesh consumed:

> It is extraordinary to see the great quantity and quality of meat – beef and mutton – that comes every day from the slaughter-houses in this city, let alone the meat that is sold at a special market held every Wednesday for meat brought in from outside the city. Truly, for those who cannot see it for themselves, it is almost impossible to believe that they could eat so much meat in one city alone. The beef is not expensive, and they roast it whole, in large pieces. They do not care as much for veal as we do.* Apart from chickens and other birds which one finds everywhere, they have many swans, much game, and rabbits and deer in abundance.[4]

*Veal was never popular in England. It was seen as wasteful (why spoil good milk on calves when there was plenty of rough pasture on which to raise beef?), suspect (why slaughter a calf unless there was something wrong with it?) and foreign (weren't veal calves bled to death, and wasn't this a Jewish method of slaughter? Hadn't veal been introduced into the land by the Normans and wasn't it popular with foreign aristocrats?). Veal production was also criticised for being cruel. This charge was already being laid at the time of Agincourt, but became increasingly influential in the eighteenth and nineteenth centuries. Mrs Beeton was speaking for many of her compatriots when she wrote that 'there was no species of slaughter practised in this country so inhuman and disgraceful as that, till very lately, employed in killing this poor animal; when, under the plea of making the flesh *white*, the calf was bled day by day, till, when the final hour came, the animal was unable to stand'. Even today, the British, who have led the campaign to improve the welfare standards for European veal, are much more likely than any of their continental neighbours to refuse to eat veal.

Paul Hentzner, a German scholar who visited England in 1598, when Shakespeare was writing *Henry V*, left a vivid portrait of a people 'powerful in the field, successful against their enemies, impatient of anything like slavery, vastly fond of great noises that fill the ear, such as the firing of cannons, drums and the ringing of bells'. Rather surprisingly, perhaps, he noted that 'they are more polite in eating than the French' but confirmed that they 'devour less bread, but more meat, which they roast to perfection'.[5] The Dutch writer Emanuel van Meteren made a similar observation a year later: the English 'feed well and delicately, and eat a great deal of meat; as Germans pass the bounds of sobriety in drinking, these do the same in eating'.[6] 'The *English* are not very Dainty', wrote Samuel Sorbière, sixty years on, 'and the greatest Lord's Tables, who do not keep *French* Cooks, are covered only with large Dishes of meat'.[7]

If the English gorged on meat did they eat a lot of beef? Noble households of the medieval, Tudor and Stuart ages tended to look down on the flesh of farm animals, preferring wild meat killed in the chase or more aristocratic birds like heron, peacock and swan. The poor, in so far as they ate meat at all, tended to eat pig, rabbit and poultry. Cows were often regarded first and foremost as working or dairy animals and culled when weak or elderly, at which point their flesh was fit only for broths and pottages. The records of Tudor churchwardens itemising expenditure on 'church ales' – fundraising celebrations hosted by local churches – suggest that roast boar and lamb, rather than roast beef, were the festive dishes of choice.[8]

Nevertheless, the enclosures in the fifteenth century, when the strip fields and commons of the feudal village were gathered into fields, most of which were given over to sheep and cattle, led to a dramatic increase in livestock. And while Tudor sources imply that more sheep were eaten than cows – a fact that would tally with the dramatic development of the wool trade during these years – enclosure also led to a jump in the production of butter, cheese and beef. The wood-pasture region of Suffolk was already a centre of dairy farming, and the Kent and Sussex Downs and marshlands of East Anglia centres of beef fattening by the beginning of the 1500s.[9]

The quantity of beef eaten, in relation to other foods in general and other meats in particular, increased further in the seventeenth century, coming at last to rival or surpass mutton. Falling wool prices were matched by a growing practice of cattle fattening, with large droves of cattle being driven from Wales and Scotland and the grazing districts of northern England to be fattened in the Midlands, East Anglia, the Home Counties and the marshes that fringed the east and south coasts from Lincoln to Romsey in Hampshire. (One east coast local described how it was annual practice for men to lay out money 'upon Heiffars and such other young ware, emptying their purses of crownes to cram the Fens with Cattell'.[10]) More than 150,000 Scottish cattle, along with a similar number of sheep, were exported to England in the 1680s, and a further 178,000 crossed the border between 1696 and 1703. As many or more came from Wales – the sight of cattle from Anglesey swimming across the Menai Straits in herds, a boat on either side to keep them in line, became a well-known local attraction. A good proportion of the Scottish animals went to supply Norwich and some of the northern wool towns, and a number of Welsh cattle were diverted to Bristol and the ports of the south coast – salt beef was standard sailor's fare. Most, however, ended up on plates in London, by 1700 the largest city in Europe and one famous for its great cattle market, Smithfield, and its teeming meat markets, butchers' shops ('the streets,' as one visitor said, 'being full of them in every direction'), its cookshops and taverns. Writing in 1698, the French traveller Henri Misson reported that 'it is common Practice, even among People of good Substance, to have a huge Piece of Roast-Beef on Sundays, of which they stuff till they can swallow no more, and eat the rest cold, without any other Victuals, the other six Days of the Week'.[11] Some twenty-five years later the Swiss traveller M. Muralt, an exceptionally penetrating commentator, corroborated the observation:

> The pleasures of the table in this happy nation may be put in the same rank as the ordinary, everyone is accustomed to good eating. They consist chiefly of a variety of puddings, Golden Pippins, which is an excellent kind of apple, delicious green oysters and roast beef, which is the favourite dish as well at the king's table as at a tradesman's; 'tis common to see one of these pieces weigh from twenty to thirty pounds . . . : and this may be said to be (as it were) the emblem of the prosperity and plenty of the English.[12]

The English were the Texans of the early modern world.

Joris Hoefnagel, *A Fête at Bermondsey, c.*1579, Hatfield House, Hertfordshire. An Elizabethan cookshop, with meat on spits clearly visible.

The English, then, ate quantities of meat, and in particular a great deal of beef. But beef also had social and cultural connotations that fostered its emergence as a patriotic symbol. For where pork and bacon were the main meats eaten by the labouring classes, and game belonged exclusively to the gentry (since the late 1300s the right to hunt game was legally restricted to men with an income of £40 a year) mutton and beef were identified, first and foremost, as the food of the yeoman farmer and his urban counterparts, the artisan and trader. These groups in turn were widely identified with the nation.

The yeoman had an important place in early modern English society. Legally defined as a freeholder who could meet the qualification for voting in parliamentary elections, the title came to be employed more widely to cover freeholders, copy holders and sometimes even tenant farmers. Descending from the free tenant, or franklin, of the medieval manor, the yeoman class swelled in size as feudal restrictions weakened, and its affluence grew. By the beginning of the 1600s, yeomen were generally living in good solid houses, furnished with glass windows, grates, chimneys, pewter tableware and down beds, luxuries almost unknown to their ancestors a hundred years before.

While some yeomen aspired to become gentlemen and educated their sons into the professions or hoped to see their daughters marry local squires, others felt a genuine pride in their station. Old Carter, a character from Thomas Dekker's *The Witch of Edmonton*, a comedy of the 1620s, corrects a man who has identified him as a fellow gentleman: 'No gentleman I; spare the Mastership, call me by my name, John Carter. Master is a title neither my father, nor his before him, were acquainted with; honest Hertfordshire yeomen; such an one am I.'[13] The yeoman had a reputation for independence, honesty and a sound knowledge of husbandry – although he employed workers, he was happy, unlike the gentleman, to get his hands dirty. His wife, or

'Goodwife' as she was formally known, took pride in her kitchen, gardens, cheeses and ale, linen and pewter.

Only a small proportion of those who now identified themselves as 'yeomen' – the term was widely used on legal documents – would have descended from soldiers who had fought at Crécy, Poitiers and Agincourt. Nevertheless, the belief that these battles had been won by yeomen archers added to the yeoman's status. Rarely did contemporary writers mention the yeomen without pointing out that it was their ancestors who 'in times past made all of France afraid'.[14]

The yeoman was not only distinguished by his skill at archery, by his sturdy good sense, warm hospitality, and, increasingly, by his comfortable home, but also by his table, especially his cheese and ale, his puddings and pies, and above all by his excellent beef and mutton. An old ballad captures his preference for four feet over two:

Talk not of goose and capon, give me good beef and bacon
And good bread and cheese now at hand:
With pudding, brawn and souse all in a farmer's house
That is living for the husband-man.[15]

Dekker's yeoman, Old Carter, boasted that his guests 'shall be welcome to bread, beer and beef – yeoman's fare. We have no kickshaws: full dishes, whole belly-fulls.' Old Trowd of Norfolk, another seventeenth-century yeoman, declared

I am proud,
And think myself as gallant in this gray,
Having my Table furnish't with good Beef,
Norfolk temes bread,*

* 'Temes' was a loaf made of flour from which the coarser bran had been removed.

And Country home bred drink,
As he that goeth in ratling Taffity.[16]

These quotes are taken from ballads and plays, but they were rooted in the real world. The moderate royalist preacher Thomas Fuller, writing at the outbreak of the English Civil War, and a great admirer of the yeomanry as 'an estate of people almost peculiar to England', boasted that 'still at our Yeoman's table you shall have as many joints as dishes; no meat disguised with strange sauces; no straggling joynt of a sheep on every side, but solid substantiall food'.[17] According to William Harrison the food of 'the artificer and husbandman . . . consisteth principally of beef and such meat as the butcher selleth, that is to say, mutton, veal, lamb, pork, etc.'.[18] Nor was the yeoman's association with beef and mutton by any means arbitrary: yeomen were found in greatest numbers in pastoral rather than arable areas – in the highlands of the North and West Country, in East Anglia, Romney Marsh and the Sussex and Kentish Downs, where the old feudal methods of production proved less viable, and so had first broken down. The middle-ranking yeoman, in other words, ate plenty of beef and mutton because he cultivated cows and sheep rather than crops.[19]

This old link between beef and yeomen provides the background to Shakespeare's lines in *Henry V* and it is the same association which must explain, at least in part, how the Yeomen of the Guard, founded by Henry VII in 1485 as a permanent military body devoted to protecting the king, became known, under the Stuarts, as 'Beef-eaters'. The name derives not, as has sometimes been claimed, from the French *buffetier* – a serving man – but from the yeoman's reputation for beef eating, and for the size of the rations of beef that the guard in fact ate. As late as 1813 the thirty yeomen on duty at St James's Palace received a ration of twenty-four pounds of beef a day, along with

Lieutenant, Ensign, and Yeomen of His Majesty's Guard of His Body.

Coronation Procession of James II, 23 April 1685. As untitled commoners, the Yeomen of the Guard, or 'Beefeaters', brought royal processions to a close.

eighteen pounds of mutton, sixteen pounds of veal, thirty-seven gallons of beer and, on Sundays, three plum puddings.[20] Assuming that the guards ate two main meals a day, that works out as the equivalent of roughly a pound of meat per meal.

The Beefeaters remain a popular tourist attraction and prominent symbol of England today; it is rare to find a London postcard rack without an image of one. Despite their name, however, it is not generally appreciated that they owed their original reputation not to their picturesque Tudor costumes or their association with the Tower of London and the Crown Jewels, but to their representing that most English of types – the valiant, patriotic, beef-eating yeoman.

2

Cooks

Englishmen understand almost better than any other people the art of properly roasting a joint which also is not to be wondered at; because the art of cooking as practised by most Englishmen does not extend much beyond roast beef and plum pudding.

Pehr Kalm, *Visit to England*, 1784

It was not only the amount of meat eaten but the way it was cooked and the things that accompanied it that marked English diet out and attracted the notice of strangers.

To begin with, the English tended to cook their meat in one of two ways. Where the Italians and the French, for instance, often fried, braised, or stewed meat, the English either boiled it (especially if it was salted) or roasted it. The latter technique, moreover, seems to have been the most common – 'English cookes', as Fynes Moryson said in 1617, 'are, in comparison with other nations, most commended for roasted meates'.[1] It was certainly the source of greatest national pride.

Nowadays if we 'roast' a joint, we cook it in the oven, but before the introduction of the gas or electric oven, roasting meat meant rotating it before a hot open fire – the word 'roast' has the same origins as 'rotate'. The technique was not as easy as it might sound. The meat had to be properly fixed to a spit to stop it slipping and the fire had to be kept at the proper temperature. The first cookery book to pay any attention to open-fire roasting, Gervase Markham's *The English Housewife* (1615), gives detailed instructions as to which meats need a gentle heat, to be 'pale and white roasted', which, like swans and peacocks, call for slow cooking and which a brisk flame.[2] While cooking, the meat had to be repeatedly basted in oil, cream or eggs and dredged with flour or breadcrumbs – 'basting upon dredging, and dredging upon basting'. Old illustrations show scullions with long spoons dipping up the juice of the meat from the dripping pan below and pouring it over the turning joint. The result, if properly done, would be quite different from a 'roast' cooked in a modern oven, which is in fact not roasted at all, but half-baked, half-braised. The outside would be puffy and crisp, the inside tender and pink. Sirloin, cut from a hindquarter of beef, was considered the best roasting joint. Two sirloins cut together as one joint formed a 'barron'. One of the patriotic legends surrounding English roast beef, firmly established by the middle of the 1600s, had it that sirloin got its name from Henry VIII, or alternatively James I, who was so impressed by a loin of beef placed before him that he raised it to the nobility as 'Sir Loin'. In fact the 'sir' derives from the French 'sur' meaning 'on' (*sur loin* – 'above the loin') but the story contributed to the identification of roast beef as England's national dish.

The most basic roasting method involved turning a simple hand-operated spit placed between metal forks that stood on the ground in front or above the fire. Such a method was used when cows were roasted whole, as they often were at market fairs or large-scale celebrations – the end of a harvest, a victorious battle, a royal coronation, the coming of age or marriage of a local nobleman.[3] The legs, head and tail of the beast were cut off, and the rounded carcass was sometimes wrapped in the fleed – the fatty inner membrane – to

Ox Roast on the Thames at the Frost Fair, woodcut, 1715–6. An ox roast on the frozen Thames, with old London Bridge in the background. A roast at a later fair in 1739–40 was provided by traders from the Strand, who bought the ox at Smithfield: one of them claimed the privilege of felling the beast on the grounds that his father had felled one roasted in 1683.

start the basting. A large animal might take over twelve hours. Locals took it in turns to rotate the spit.

This technique could also be used to cook smaller joints indoors. Hand roasting, however, made for tiring and time-consuming work, and the popularity of roast meat was such that even fairly modest households often owned more sophisticated, labour-saving devices.

In one popular alternative to turning the meat by hand, a small dog worked a wooden treadmill harnessed to the spit. A treatise on dogs from 1536 confirms that dogwheels were well established:

> A certain dog in kitchen service [is] excellent. For when any meat is to be roasted they go into a wheel, which, they turning about with the weight of their bodies so diligently look to their business that no drudge or scullion can do the feat more cunningly.[4]

Visiting Bristol a century later, the Cornishman Peter Mundy reported that there was 'scarce a house that hath not a dogge to turn the spitte in a little wooden wheele', and they stayed in use as late as 1800 in country districts.[5]

The evidence of probate inventories, however – the list of a man's possessions at the time of his death – suggests that dogwheels were never as common as weight-driven machines or 'roasting jacks'. The modern roasting jack came from Renaissance Italy: Leonardo da Vinci

Thomas Rowlandson, *The Inn Kitchen at Newcastle Emlyn, Cardiganshire,* showing dogwheel at work.

left an early design for one in his notebooks. By the end of the sixteenth century, they were established in England and spread rapidly over the next century, when they became one of the most expensive items owned by many households. A Swedish naturalist, Pehr Kalm, who visited England in the 1740s, observed that 'Meat jacks, or spits, they have in every house in England. They are turned by a weight, which is drawn up as often as it has run down.'[6] They were so popular that jack-making became a specialised branch of metalworking. Often the line of the jack was passed up into the ceiling or down into a basement, to increase the time it took to complete its fall: Dr Johnson recalled that his family home in Lichfield had 'a little dark room behind the kitchen where the jack weight fell through a hole in the floor'.[7]

Finally, the smoke jack offered a third option. Once again, Leonardo had demonstrated the principle of harnessing the hot upward draught of the chimney flue, although it was not until the end of the early eighteenth century that smoke jacks, operated by large smoke-propelled wings inserted in the chimney, became at all common in England. Where dogwheels and weight jacks were most useful in turning small- or medium-sized pieces of meat, smoke jacks came into their own for cooking large joints before a big blazing fire – and English joints often reached weights of sixty pounds or more. For this reason dogwheels and weight jacks were usually found in domestic kitchens, and smoke jacks in larger households or inns and taverns, although some kitchens possessed two or even three different types of turning device, used as the occasion demanded.

Even in the seventeenth century, the English took pride in the plainness and honesty of their cooking. Meat was generally served simply with its own juices, or 'gravy', rather than with the fancy stock-based reductions increasingly fashionable in France – hence Voltaire's quip that the English had a hundred religions but only one sauce. It was, however, typically accompanied by other things that became almost inextricably linked with it, and took on some of its symbolism, including mustard and horseradish.

The mustard plant was native to Western Europe and had been exploited by the Romans, and horseradish was widely used in the medieval kitchen, but their English preparation was distinctive. Cooks in central and northern Italy typically used mustard in making *mostarda di frutta* – a sweet preserve of candied fruits, sugar and mustard oil, still eaten with boiled meat today – and the French ate it mild, preserved with vinegar and honey or sugar, but Britons liked it strong and were proud of the fact. (An anti-Dutch print of the 1660s dismisses Holland as 'A Land of Bog / To Breed up Hogs, / Good pork with *English* mustard'.)*[8] The English mustard trade first arose in Tewkesbury, Gloucestershire, in the sixteenth century.[9] In Shakespeare's *Henry IV, Pt 2*, Falstaff describes someone as possessing a wit 'as thicke as Tewkesburie mustard'. The mustard seed was ground, blended with horseradish, and formed into balls that could be broken up and mixed with vinegar or wine. These balls kept fairly well and were sold throughout the country. The invention of powdered mustard in the course of the eighteenth century led to an even stronger version.

As with mustard, so with horseradish. Where in France the horseradish root was generally combined with cream and lemon, in England it was mixed with vinegar: 'Take Roots of Horse-radish scraped clean, and lay them to soak in fair-water for an hour' says a cookbook of 1669. 'Then rasp them upon a Grater, and you have them all tender spungy Pap. Put Vinegar to it, and a very little sugar, not so

* In *The Accomplisht Cook* (the first full-scale English cookery book) of 1660 Robert May, who had lived in France and England, gives instructions for both French and English mustard: the first incorporates honey and cinnamon, the second nothing but 'strong wine vinegar'.

much as to be tasted, but to quicken (by contrariety) the taste of the other.'[10] By the middle of the eighteenth century roast beef and horseradish were a well-established pairing. 'Take up your meat and garnish your dish with nothing but Horse-raddish' ends a typical roast beef recipe from the 1740s.[11]

In addition to these condiments, two other accompaniments also stand out. The first was pudding, which, foreigners noted, the English loved almost as much as beef:

> Blessed be he that invented pudding! For it is a manna that hits the palates of all sorts of people; a manna better than that of the wilderness, because the people are never weary of it . . . Give an English man a pudding and he will think it a noble treat in any part of the world![12]

To say, in the seventeenth century, that something 'came in pudding time' was to imply that it was well timed.[13]

'The pudding', as Henri Misson observed, 'is a thing very difficult to describe', and he was right. Nevertheless, pudding historians tell us that, very roughly, a pudding is a confection of some form of starch and fat, cooked with meat, vegetable or fruit, encased in some form of a skin or shell and generally either boiled or baked. The word derives from the Latin *botellus*, meaning sausage, and is first cousin to the French *boudin* (a form of sausage) as well as the Portuguese *pudim* and the Spanish *pudding* – both closer to the French sweet *flan*. In the Middle Ages, a pudding was always enclosed in stomach or intestinal lining, although it might contain oatmeal as well as meat, or sweet ingredients as well as savoury – the Scottish national dish haggis is, basically, a medieval pudding. In England, however, puddings encased in skin evolved into puddings baked in a dish in the oven or wrapped in a pudding cloth (a late sixteenth-century invention) and boiled.

Misson stressed their range and variety: a pudding might include oatmeal, flour, barley or bread; butter, suet or bone marrow; dried peas, carrots, pears or apples; 'they bake them in an oven, they boil them with meat, they make them fifty several ways'. He might have added that they also varied from place to place. 'Hogs pudding', made from barley and pig offal, was popular in the West Country, black

Paul Sandby, *Hot Pudding Seller*, 1759. The seller's barrow probably contained hot charcoals in a metal box, to keep his puddings hot.

pudding (blood sausage) in Lancashire and 'pease pudding' in the North East. They are still eaten today.

For all their variety, however – and Mrs Beeton's *Book of Household Management* of 1861 contains over a hundred pudding recipes and variations – two puddings in particular gradually established themselves as national favourites. One was the plum pudding, which developed in the course of the seventeenth century from a loose pottage, made from chopped beef or mutton, onions and dried fruit, and served before or with the meat course, to a firm, sweeter, spherical pudding boiled in a cloth, made from suet, dried fruit and sugar, and increasingly eaten at the end of the meal. A particularly sweet and rich version of this dish accompanied roast beef on Christmas Day, and the English and their imperial offshoots in Australia, New Zealand, Canada, and elsewhere, still eat it on that occasion. Another favourite, of later provenance, was a batter and dripping pudding, created by placing a partly cooked pancake beneath a joint of meat as it roasted before an open fire. The earliest published recipe dates from the 1730s, although it was another ten years before it began to be identified as 'Yorkshire pudding'.*

If the English ate mustard, horseradish and pudding with their meat, they tended to drink ale, beer or cider. The English upper classes, it is true, had drunk wine since Roman times, some of it made from vines grown in Britain – England having a warmer climate in those days – but most was imported from the Continent, especially

*English puddings were close cousins – often virtually inseparable – from another immensely popular and wide-ranging English speciality: the pie. Often, as in steak and kidney pudding and steak and kidney pie, the ingredients were almost the same, only the casing and the cooking method being different. The close connection between the two types is illustrated by 'Christmas Pye' which according to Misson, was 'eaten everywhere' in the seventeenth century; made of 'Neats-tongues, Chicken, Eggs, Sugar, Raisins, Lemon, Orange Peel and various Kinds of Spicery', it is clearly a forerunner of Christmas pudding.

from the vineyards of Bordeaux, which was under English rule from the twelfth to the middle of the fifteenth century, and later (after the introduction, in the early eighteenth century, of punitive taxes aimed at curtailing French imports) from Portugal. Even here, however, national tastes proved distinctive. The English liked their claret fortified with stronger Rhône wines, and their Portuguese wines fortified with spirits – hence 'port'. The German traveller J.W. von Archenholz observed of English drinkers, 'they like everything that is powerful and heavy'.[14]

The English climate, however, had always been better suited to ale, or, in the South and South West, to cider, and these remained, at least among all but the aristocracy, the drinks of choice. In *Henry V* Shakespeare has his French commanders disparage England's 'barley broth', but English patriots insisted on its superiority to France's grape juice. 'For your wyne', John Coke told the French in the middle of the 1500s, 'we have good-ale, bere, metheghelen, sydre, and perry, being more wholesome beverages for us than your wynes, which maketh your people drunken, also prone and apte to all filthy pleasures and lustes.'[15] Most medieval villages possessed an alehouse, its ale generally supplied by the manor, which claimed a monopoly on the commercial production of alcohol. As the tenant farmers and villagers became independent, ale was brewed in almost every home. By the middle of the 1600s, quite substantial brewhouses – special structures, usually abutting the main residence, devoted to brewing – were common even in small farmers' and skilled artisans' homes. The frontispiece of the *Dictionarium Domesticum*, a popular household manual published in 1736, represents brewing as an essential housewife's skill, along with open-fire cooking, butter making, care of the larder and baking.

Beer – ale made from hops – was introduced from the Continent early in the fifteenth century, and at first was not welcomed. The

The five skills of the housewife, from Nathan Bailey, *Dictionarium Domesticum*, 1736. From top-left, clockwise: butter-making, brewing, care of the stillroom or larder, baking, open-fire cooking. Note the weight-driven roasting jack to the left of the fire.

medical writer Andrew Boorde, writing in the 1540s, cautioned that beer was 'the naturall drynke for a Dutche man. And nowe of late days it is moche vsed in Englande to the detriment of many Englysshe men', and similar complaints could still be heard in the mid-seventeenth century.[16] Beer's popularity, however, spread, especially in the towns, in part no doubt because it goes off less quickly than ale, owing to the preservative quality of the resin in hops. A French traveller, visiting a Cambridge clergyman in 1672, commented on the obligation of drinking 'two or three pots of beer during our parley; for no kind of business is transacted in England without the intervention of pots of beer'.[17] Eighteenth-century drinkers had a particular liking for 'porter', a sweet dark beer, about twice the strength of modern bitter. Said to have first been brewed by one Ralph Harwood, a London brewer, in 1724, it probably acquired its name from its popularity with London porters. The great Benjamin Franklin, who worked as a printer in London in the 1720s, remembered his companions drinking six pints of the stuff in the course of the working day. More substantial than ordinary beer, it was often used to lubricate puddings and went particularly well with roast meat.

3

Fricassees

October 17 Sunday [1802]
Very weak this Morning, scarce able to put on my Cloaths and with great difficulty, get down Stairs with help. Mr Dade read Prayers & Preached this Morning at Weston Church – Nancy at Church. Mr and Mrs Custance & Lady Bacon at Church. Dinner to day, Roast Beef & c.

The last entry in Parson Woodforde's *Diary*

BY THE EARLY 1700s the English had developed a distinctive diet, centred around roast meat and gravy, fiery condiments, hearty puddings and pies and fortified wine, ale, beer and porter. This characterisation, however, only takes us so far. To get a fuller sense of the personality of English cooking – to grasp it in all its cultural significance – it needs to be compared to that of France, since the development of French cuisine throws into sharp relief some important features of its English counterpart.

French and English cooking had their origins in a common medieval tradition, yet by the end of the seventeenth century the two had grown apart, as French cuisine became increasingly refined and its English counterpart remained relatively 'backward' or (according to your point of view) 'honest'. For generations, food historians repeated the claim that the development of a distinctively French culinary tradition could be traced back to the 1530s, and the arrival of the Italian Catherine de' Medici in France as wife of the future Henri II. Renaissance Italy had established a sophisticated court culture, marked by new humanist ideals of politeness, learning and artistic expression. In the process Italian cooking lost much of its medieval roughness and Catherine and her large retinue of cooks now transported – or so the argument went – the new style of courtly cooking to France.

Recent historians, however, have argued that Catherine's role was much exaggerated: the interchange of ideas and people between France and Italy began long before her arrival and continued after her death.[1] This is doubtless true, but a new sort of cooking did emerge in the Renaissance courts of the Italian city states and it had a marked effect on the food eaten by the French aristocracy. And as France established itself over the next two centuries as the leading arbiter of courtly taste, its cooking became ever more refined. The kitchens of France's great magnates and aristocrats, like the Princes of the Blood, the Cardinals Richelieu, Mazarin and de Retz, or the duc de Rohan, sought to outdo each other and rival those of the royal court. These in turn set standards emulated by those lower down the social pile. Result: the birth of French *haute cuisine*. Contrary to popular belief, the high standard of French cooking owes more to social snobbery than peasant good taste.

By the beginning of the 1700s French cooking had developed many of the characteristics with which it is still associated today. Sweet and savoury ingredients were fairly rigidly separated; the exotic spices of old had largely been supplanted by local seasonings, especially parsley and thyme; pastry was thin and light; vegetables, often fried in batter or sautéed in stock, were treated as delicacies in their own right; eggs were exploited not only to bind puddings and fillings, but as the basis for delicately flavoured omelettes and pancakes with the dainty name of *quelquechoses,* and for cakes and biscuits. Perhaps most significantly, the wide range of roasted mammals and birds of the medieval table – the whales, porcupines, peacocks and herons – had given way to a focus on the meats we still eat today: chiefly poultry, venison, game, lamb, pork and beef. These were no longer so often roasted as plied with delicate stuffings and baked in an oven ('bisques' or 'terrines'), or stewed in stock and then served with a thickened stock-based sauce ('ragouts' or 'fricassees'). It was in the seventeenth century, in fact, that stock emerged as the basic building block of French meat and fish cookery – used in braising, stewing and making sauces, but also as a foundation for smooth cream-based soups. Revealingly, the opening recipe in the cookery book generally accepted as first showing the recognisable beginning of modern French cuisine, La Varenne's *Le Cuisinier françois* of 1651, is for *bouillon,* or stock.

This process of refinement continued apace in the eighteenth century, the first decades of which saw something of a culinary revolution: the emergence of a self-proclaimed *nouvelle cuisine.* Late seventeenth-century French court cooking – the cooking that came out of Louis XIV's kitchens at Versailles – was essentially baroque. The centrepiece of the meal tended to be a tureen piled high with a pyramid of different meats and exotic garnishes – sweetbread, artichoke hearts, nuts – swimming in a rich stock-based sauce, a complicated creation that could, according to one cookery book, take half an hour to construct.[2] In the course of the 1720s and 1730s, however, this gave way to a new style of smaller dishes offering a single dominant flavour and concentrated sauces.

These changes in the way food was prepared were accompanied by developments in the way it was served. In the France of Louis XIV, pride of place was given to the elaborate court dinner involving massive tables intricately laid out and serving dozens of diners. Cookery books of the period pay almost as much attention to the arrangement of dishes on the table as they do to the dishes themselves. Louis XIV's successor, however, Philippe, duc d'Orléans, Regent for the young Louis XV, fancied himself something of a cook and gourmet and began a fashion for small supper parties, at which host and guests took turns at the stove. The *souper intime,* where jokes could be made, plots hatched and partners seduced in the privacy of a small, elegant salon, remained an aristocratic favourite until the Revolution.

The contrast with English cookery was marked. The English tended to adapt, rather than renounce, medieval practices; they continued, as we have seen, to eat a great deal of roast or boiled meat, and they served this with gravy or pickles, mustard, horseradish, and other, often sweet, accompaniments, rather than with the new rich sauces so popular in France. Where even modest seventeenth-century French kitchens were often equipped with brick stoves and copper pots for the preparation of soups, stews and sauces, the English largely made do with their beloved roasting jacks. Similarly, English puddings and pies, so heavy when compared to France's delicate omelettes, crêpes and tarts, often combined sweet and savoury ingredients. And where the French made extensive use of sautéed onions, garlic, and wild mushrooms, eaten on their own or combined with meat ('there are scarcely any ragouts without them', as one English tourist observed), the English preferred plainer boiled vegetables, like 'cabbage, carrots, turnips, . . . served well peppered and salted and swimming in butter'.[3]

The cooking enjoyed by the English upper classes was, of course, richer and more elaborate than that eaten by their inferiors. Yet by comparison with France, where cuisine was used to advertise and entrench class distinctions, many English gentlemen prided themselves on their plain, unaffected English tastes. Roast beef might have been most closely identified with the yeoman, but it was enjoyed by those higher up – and lower down – the social pyramid too. The great Whig politician Anthony Ashley Cooper, the first Earl of Shaftesbury, left an unforgettable description of a Dorset neighbour of the 1630s. Henry Hastings Esq., the second son of an earl, was, with his ancient green woollen clothes and ferocious manners, very much a country gentleman of the old school. His house contained only two books, the King James Bible and Foxe's *Book of Martyrs*, but overflowed with hawks, cats and dogs, hunting poles, arrows, crossbows and stonebows. Guests 'found beef, pudding and small-beer in great plenty'. The house chapel served as a pantry and 'was never wanting of a cold chine of beef, venison-pasty, gammon or a great apple-pye with thick crust extremely baked'. The floor was strewn with foxes' skins and marrowbones.[4] His near contemporary Sir William Walter showed himself a little more modern minded. He went so far as to employ a French cook on his country estate after his marriage, but he insisted that he make traditional food. After six months the cook asked leave to return to London, complaining 'a piece of Beefe, a piece of Mutton and a pudding; what needs that a French Cooke?'[5]

The gentry's taste for plain country fare continued into the eighteenth century. Squire Western, from Henry Fielding's novel *Tom Jones* – an inspired caricature of the bone-headed, town-hating, Tory squire – appears to eat little but vast joints of roast beef and plum pudding.

The country parson and diarist James Woodforde loved his food and did not disapprove when friends served a 'very genteel dinner' that included 'Soals and Lobster Sauce' and a 'Fillet of Veal rosted with Morells and Trufles'.[6] At home, however, he eschewed fancy French-style dishes for a diet of roast mutton, pork, beef, poultry and game,

Thomas Rowlandson, *A Good Meal,* Private Collection. Rowlandson depicts an ideal-type Englishman being served by an ideal-type Englishwoman. Port, madeira and claret are on display in the tub by the table, but judging from the foam pouring from his vessel, he is drinking beer, the proper accompaniment to roast beef.

boiled gammons and tongues, pease puddings and fruit pies. Roast beef and plum pudding were special favourites, regardless of the season. On 14 May 1782 Woodforde served four neighbours a typical dinner of '4 Spring Chickens boiled and a Ham, part of a Rump of Beef boiled, a leg of Mutton rosted with sweet Sauce and a boiled plumb pudding'. On 3 December of the same year his guests dined on 'Salt Fish, a Leg of Mutton boiled and capers, a Knuckle of Veal, a Piggs Face, a fine Surloin of Beef rosted and plenty of plumb Pudding'. Three weeks later, Christmas was celebrated with the traditional roast beef, plumb pudding and mince pies.

Even where the upper classes developed a taste for French cooking, they took a certain pride in being able to offer their workers and dependants honest English fare, one for which they, like their workers, generally felt a real affection. When Sir Michael Newton's wife gave birth to an heir in 1732, he gave 'a splendid Entertainment' at Leominster: '30 Dozen of Wine, 10 Hogshead of Cyder, an Ox roasted whole in the Street, and 20s. to every Publick-house in Town'. When he finished the harvest in 1768, Francis Prior of Ufton, Berkshire, 'Gave all the people that work'd that day their supper and plenty of Ale and I intend if please God I live till the next harvest and remain in the same mind I now am to provide on this occasion a large Round of Beef'.[7] In September 1776 Woodforde recorded that after being 'Very busy all day with my Barley . . . my Harvest Men dined here to day, gave them some Beef and some plumb Pudding and as much liquor as they would drink'.

Thus in the countryside, and even in London, the centre of fashion, gentlemen were often seen eating in taverns and cookshops – something quite unthinkable in France. Here is the famous courtier and libertine, Lord Rochester, versifying the praises of the roast beef served at the (fittingly titled) Bull, a well-known London inn:

Our own plain fare, and the best terse [claret] the Bull
Affords, I'll give you and your bellies full.
As for French kickshaws, sillery [a white wine] and champagne
Ragouts and fricasees, in throth, w'have none.
Here's a good dinner towards, thought I, when straight,
Up comes a piece of beef, full horseman's weight.[8]

It says much about the difference between French and English cooking, that whereas French cookery books were written exclusively by male chefs, generally trained at a court and offering guidance in the court tradition, many English cookery books, even in the eighteenth century, were written by women and aimed at 'housewives' – that is women in charge of running a relatively small household or estate.[9] So while eighteenth-century Frenchmen wrote books like *Le Cuisinier royal* or *La Cuisine de la cour*, English bestsellers included Mary Kettibly's *A Collection of above Three Hundred Receipts* (1714), Eliza Smith's *The Compleat Housewife* (1727), Elizabeth Moxon's *English Housewifery* (1749), Elizabeth Raffald's *The Experienced English Housekeeper* (1769) and the most successful of all, Hanna Glasse's *The Art of Cookery Made Plain and Easy* (1747), the first cookery book to offer a recipe for 'Yorkshire pudding'. And where French cookbooks tended to represent their recipes as fashionable and innovative – dishes were often labelled *à la mode* – English ones advertised their recipes as traditional. The first French cookbook to be directed specifically to modest female cooks, *Cuisinère Bourgeoisie*, was not published until 1746; its author, Menon, was a man trained in the aristocratic tradition.

The difference between the paths taken by French and English cooking was evident to any well-travelled contemporary observer. Looking at it from the distance of three centuries, however, a certain irony emerges. France is still associated with cooking, but nowadays the cooking that it identifies with tends to be that of the *terroir* – the land. Champions of French food see themselves as defending age-old methods of production and exchange and the communities that contain them, against the forces of 'rationalising', homogenising globalisation. These days Britain, by contrast, hardly defines itself in food terms at all. Characteristic farmhouse cooking survives in some households and a few restaurants but generally speaking British food has lost contact with the land. It is processed and uniform: Tesco sells the same products in Penzance as it does in Inverness and most of that product will have been manufactured on standardised, technological lines.

But this represents a marked turnaround, for once it was French food that was distinguished by its artificiality. It built on new technologies and experimented with new methods; it was forward looking and high-tech. Louis XIV's gardeners were famous for producing peas in April, his cooks for producing ices in the height of summer. The great French chefs of the period claimed, as they have done ever since, that their innovations were creating a more 'natural' cuisine – that they were bringing out the native essences of ingredients and arranging them in natural harmonies – but these claims were dismissed by English cooks. It was English cooking, they contended, that was closer to nature. It was traditional, seasonal and easy to prepare. The reversal had much to do with the emergence, on the one hand, of the French peasantry as an important political and cultural force in the nineteenth century, and, on the other, with the rapid industrialisation and urbanisation of Britain. But it would have surprised and unsettled Stuart and Hanoverian Britons, who liked to believe that it was their cooking, and not France's, that was closer to nature.

4

Patriots

For my own part, I look upon it as a peculiar Blessing that I was born an Englishman.

The *Spectator*, letter 103, 28 June 1711

IN 1747 ROBERT CAMPBELL issued the first edition of *The London Tradesman*, a detailed guide to the capital's apprenticeships, aimed at modest tenant farmers, artisans and workers, wanting to place their children in a London trade. For the most part, Campbell stuck to his task in a business-like way, describing the length of apprenticeships, conditions of work, and financial rewards of the various trades – so making his book a mine of useful information to modern-day historians. He was writing at a time of intense Gallophobia – France and England were at war again – and when it came to writing about the trade of the cook, he could not resist a blow in support of English cooking:

In the Days of good Queen Elizabeth, when mighty Roast Beef was the Englishman's Food; our Cookery was plain and simple as our Manners; it was not then a Science or Mistery, and required no Conjuration to please the Palates of our greatest Men. But we have of late Years, refined ourselves out of that simple Taste, and conformed our Palates to Meats

> and Drinks dressed after the French Fashion: The natural Taste of Fish or Flesh is become nauseous to our fashionable Stomach; we abhor that anything should appear at our Tables in its native Properties; all the Earth, from both the Poles, the most distant and different Climates, must be ransacked for Spices, Pickles and Sauces, not to relish but to disguise our food. Fish, when it has passed the Hands of a French Cook, is no more Fish; it has neither the Taste, Smell, nor Appearance of Fish. It, and every thing else, is dressed in Masquerade, seasoned with slow Poisons, and every Dish pregnant with nothing, but the Seeds of Diseases both chronick and acute.[1]

Campbell's invective suggests that the picture sketched so far – a picture of two distinct national traditions neatly divided by the Channel – leaves something out. Far from being eaten only in France, French food had long been favoured by the English upper classes, and this caused deep dismay among patriots lower down the social scale. English cooking, in fact, developed in no small part in contradistinction to the fancy French style so popular with England's 'people of quality'. There *were* two distinct traditions, French and English, with all the contrasts already depicted. But the French one was making increasing inroads into England, and the English tradition of plain country cooking – of roast beef, plum pudding and porter – developed in part by defining itself against the French.

The fashion for continental food tended to be channelled through the court (hardly surprising given that all the Stuart kings – James I, Charles I, Charles II, James II – were descended from or married to continental, Catholic royalty), but, as in France, the new style soon spread outwards and downwards. Ironically Puritan victory in the Civil War of the 1640s worked, ultimately, to encourage the spread of aristocratic foreign taste, for many royalists were forced to take refuge in France, and came back with a taste for French court cooking and often with French cooks who knew how to prepare it. Samuel Pepys' famous diary provides a contemporary record of the process. Immediately after Charles II's return to England from Holland, Pepys' patrons, the Earl and Countess of Sandwich, embraced the newly fashionable style. After dining with them, Pepys quoted the earl as 'very high how he would have a French cooke and a Master of his Horse . . . ; which methought was strange, but he is become a perfect Courtier'. A few months later, Pepys himself exchanged the English style of dress, with cloak and rapier, for the French coat and sword: French dishes too began to make a regular appearance at his table.[2]

The trend continued in the next century, although with this important difference. Whereas in the seventeenth century the taste for courtly cooking was disseminated from the Stuart court outwards, the Germanic Hanoverian courts of George I, George II and George III were famously unstylish. Instead, French cooking became closely associated with the great Whig grandees who dominated the government and the country; Robert Walpole, the Duke of Newcastle and the Dukes of Richmond and Bedford, Lord Chesterfield and Lord Albemarle, to mention only a few, all employed top French chefs.[3] Fashionable aristocrats wrote regularly to their connections in France – ambassadors, expatriates, French friends and relations – begging them to find French cooks for their service, for 'nothing', as the Duke of Newcastle wrote during one such quest, 'is of greater importance here than the reputation of having a good cook'. When Emily Lennox, daughter to the second Duke of Richmond and newly married to the Earl of Kildare, arrived in Ireland in 1747, she was horrified to discover that there were no specialist chefs – 'everybody's housekeeper is their confectioner'. She wrote to her father, recently appointed Ambassador to Versailles, asking him to secure a French chef, and he dutifully added this item to his list of 'things to be gott in Paris'.[4] Indeed, many of the leading, most highly paid French chefs of the period, including Pierre Cloué, Vincent La Chapelle and M. La Grange, worked in England or for English aristocrats living abroad. French culinary historians have been slow to acknowledge it, but the truth is that *nouvelle cuisine* was almost as much an English aristocratic phenomenon as it was a French one. La Varenne's ground-breaking court manual of 1651 was translated into English within three years of its first appearance in France, but Vincent La Chapelle's *The Modern Cook,* one of the bibles of the new style, appeared in English in 1733, two years *before* it was published in France.

But popularity alone cannot explain the strength of Campbell's and others' opposition to French cuisine. Why did French court cooking seem so objectionable? To answer that question we need to step back a moment and place Englishmen's fears about their food in a broader context. Englishmen disapproved of French food as much as they did because they saw its forward march as epitomising broader, still more pernicious changes. It was not just roast beef and plum pudding that were endangered. Alien forces – a new corruption – seemed to threaten their ancient liberties, livelihoods and customs. England itself was in peril.

Nations are obscure, elusive things – 'We know what they are when you don't ask us', to paraphrase the nineteenth-century liberal Walter Bagehot, 'but we can not very quickly explain or define them.'[5] It is hard to say exactly when the English nation first emerged, who was included in it, or what its defining attributes were. Nevertheless, by the end of the seventeenth century, the English possessed a comparatively strong sense of national identity. Stuart England was almost alone in Europe, for instance, in having a developed calendar of national as distinct from religious holidays, although the two were, in the minds of most Englanders, very nearly inseparable.

Myriad factors contributed to the English sense of themselves as a people apart. The decline of feudalism in the country in the late medieval period and the expansion of trade in the cities loosened local ties and master–servant relations, and created a new class of independent gentlemen, yeomen, lawyers, merchants and craftsmen, who identified themselves with the nation. The Hundred Years War with France (1337–1453) was fought largely in the name of the 'King of England', rather than the English nation, but it worked to sharpen national consciousness, especially in those soldiers who fought the French. The invention of the printing press at the end of the fifteenth century, and the increase in literacy that it encouraged, fostered the development of a national language and literature, which in turn encouraged a feeling of common belonging. A strong tradition of common law dating back to at least the Magna Carta and the development, in the course of the seventeenth century, of the belief that England was governed by 'an ancient constitution' that guaranteed the 'rights of the freeborn Englishman', engendered a sense of political community.

But it was Protestantism that played perhaps the most important role in forging English identity.[6] The Reformation was not always helpful in cementing a sense of nationhood; religious conflict tore France, the Netherlands and the German states apart and threatened to do the same to England. Elizabeth I's long reign, however, brought this chapter of English history to an end. Her tolerant Protestantism, with its reluctance to 'make windows into men's souls', prevented too much discord between conservative Anglicans and radical Puritans. At the same time, the Catholic menace, first from within, in the form of Mary Queen of Scots and her supporters, and then from without, in the form of the Spanish Armada, provided the nation with a sense of purpose; England defined itself against the threat from Rome. The queen herself became a cult figure, the living fusion of nation and Church, the virgin bride of every Englishman. In 1576 the Church added her accession day to its select calendar of Holy Days, in effect making the anniversary of her coronation a public holiday. And anti-popery was just as vital a force in seventeenth-century England as it had been in the England of Elizabeth. The fateful decision to take up arms against Charles I in 1642 (the beginning of the Civil War), his execution in 1649, and the deposing of James II in 1688 – each act in flagrant violation of widely proclaimed monarchist principles – were all justified in terms of the need to protect Britain from the Catholic anti-Christ.

If the English had already, by the beginning of the 1700s, evolved a fairly distinct sense of themselves as a people apart, developments over the next fifty or sixty years entrenched English national consciousness and intensified English xenophobia.[7] This period, stretching roughly from the Glorious Revolution of 1688 to the end of the Seven Years War in 1763 is often described as one of growing 'commerce', 'politeness' or 'stability'. The replacing of the Catholic James II by the Protestant William III and the formal exclusion of all Catholics that followed, decided, apparently once and for all, the long-running conflicts between divine right monarchists and constitutionalists in favour of the latter. The fire that had fuelled decades of violent religious and political conflict had been extinguished, even if its embers continued to glow.

To the people on the ground, however, the eighteenth century seemed hardly less tumultuous than the seventeenth. Far from feeling secure, they were anxious and embattled. To begin with, it was by no means as obvious to contemporaries as it is to historians that the 1688 settlement would last. Important steps were taken to protect the mixed, Protestant constitution; the Act of Settlement of 1701 forbade a Catholic from occupying the throne; the Act of Union of 1707 pulled Scotland – long a hotbed of religious and civil conflict – into what it was hoped would prove a stabilising English embrace. But a part of the country – no one knew how significant a part – remained unreconciled to the new order. This included most Catholics, especially in Ireland and Scotland, but also many Anglican Tories, who remained loyal to the 'king over the water', either as a matter of principle or because they disliked the alliance of foreign monarchs, Whig ministers, corrupt placemen, grasping merchants and upstart Dissenters who, as they saw it, were running the country into ruin. And the absolutist Catholic cause had powerful support in the form of France, the major land power of the day. France and Britain were at war between 1689 and 1697 (Nine Years War), 1702 and 1713 (War of Spanish Succession), 1739 and 1748 (War of Austrian Succession) and 1756 and 1763 (Seven Years War) – and in all but the last the French fought not just for strategic or economic advantage, but to restore Catholic Stuart rule to Britain. The French also backed the formidable Stuart-led, Scottish-based uprisings in 1715 and 1745. We know that the Protestant regime survived these challenges but that this would be the case was far from obvious at the time. Little wonder that politics was haunted by rumours of Catholic spies and Stuart plots, by assassination panics and invasion scares.

French military ambition abroad and Jacobite conspiracy at home were only the most obvious threats. Unsettling economic, political and cultural changes also gave patriots reason to feel that the England of old was slipping away. The Glorious Revolution of 1688 marked the beginning of an extraordinarily rapid economic transformation, as London gave birth to many of the financial institutions and practices of the modern capitalist economy, including a national bank, large public debt, and an extensive market in stocks. England had entered on what Daniel Defoe called its 'age of projects'.[8] Landed gentry, smaller city merchants and independent tradesmen, many of whom saw their incomes decline during this period, disapproved of these innovations. They did not understand how they worked – hardly anybody did – but they disliked the easy money they offered to the growing class of parasitical financiers or 'money men', and despaired at seeing their taxes used to repay loans taken out at exorbitant rates of interest. Their enmity was only deepened by the fact that so many stockholders and moneylenders were wealthy metropolitan aristocrats with close ties to the government, or foreigners – mainly Dutchmen or Jews. Stock-jobbers were described as 'ravens', 'monsters', 'pickpockets', and the Royal Exchange as a '*Den of Thieves*'.[9]

These changes in English financial practices were mirrored by changes in the working of government – changes similarly anathema to the outlook of upright, freedom-loving Englishmen. As patriots complained, the king or his ministers, while paying lip service to the liberal principles of 1688, soon found ways around them, ensuring that power rested not with honest beef-eating men of independent means in the counties and the boroughs, but with corrupt ministers, government stooges, moneymen and other vicious, fricassee-consuming London types.

Again, these changes can be traced, in part, to the period's vast and expensive wars, which increased the size of government, so increasing its power over Parliament. At the same time, the cost of fighting elections rose, and the size of the franchise fell, changes that similarly worked to strengthen the government's hand. These developments, largely set in motion under William III, snowballed under the rule of the first two Georges, or more accurately, under Robert Walpole,

Prime Minister from 1721 to 1742, and his successors, Henry Pelham and his brother, the Duke of Newcastle.

Walpole, a politician of genius, used his talents to spin an extraordinarily far-reaching web of patronage: every appointment in Church and state, no matter how insignificant, was made conditional on support for the 'Prime-Minister' or his followers. This unrivalled empire of dependency created something like a one-party state, administered by a network of rich aristocratic families, with Walpole at its head. The Houses of Parliament were packed with relatives. Election was often a formality – the constituency of Gatton in Surrey had six voters. Important sections of the country, including much of the poorer landed gentry and smaller merchants and tradesmen, not to mention the popular classes, remained hostile to the new order. Most of the great writers and intellectuals of the period – Swift, Pope, Gay, Fielding and Bolingbroke – agitated against it. But it was part of Walpole's genius to marginalise and divide this opposition. The English oligarchy had come of age.

Finally, these economic and political developments were accompanied by unsettling changes in culture and consumption: with the new money went new ways of spending it. These could be seen all around the country, in the mushrooming of great landed houses and gardens (the biggest of which – Blenheim, Castle Howard, Chatsworth, Stowe – outrivalled the royal palaces), and in the proliferation of substantial suburban villas and handsome townhouses. It was evident in the introduction, even into fairly modest homes, of china and glassware, cotton sheets and upholstered chairs, silk stockings and fashionable hats, sugar, tea and coffee. It was manifest in the development of spa towns and seaside resorts, like Bath and Brighton, given over to leisure and pleasure, as well as in the appearance, even in ordinary working towns, of parks, theatres, ballrooms and libraries, art galleries and racecourses.

The changes afoot were nowhere more evident than in the capital. The London to which Charles II returned in 1660 was already one of the biggest cities in the world. Nevertheless its centre remained within the old medieval city boundaries, a huddle of winding lanes, narrow alleys and crooked buildings. The rebuilding that followed the Fire of London in 1666 transformed the capital. Streets were widened, modern docks constructed, wooden buildings replaced with less combustible brick and new churches erected under the supervision of Christopher Wren. The most dramatic developments, however, took place to the west, where the green spaces that had divided the City from Westminster, the centre of government, were developed into the elegant, aristocratic promenades of Bloomsbury, Soho, Mayfair and Marylebone, lined with tall townhouses and large palaces, all within strolling distance of the royal parks. By 1750, London was the biggest city in the Christian world, and one of the most splendid.

It was not just the architecture that was different. London was developing into a new kind of city – one designed for pleasure. Charles II and his gay, licentious court had set the tone in the 1660s. The king encouraged writers and wits, licensed theatres, bought vast quantities of paintings, seduced women, and sauntered in the royal parks. Under his successors, the vogue for pleasure spread from the court to the West End. For the first time people moved to London not just to work but to enjoy themselves – to *live*. The city's diversions, indeed, seemed endless. There were parks – like Hyde Park, Green Park and, above all, St James's, to name but three – where people of fashion showed off their ornaments. There were coffee houses and clubs, theatres, print sellers and art galleries, where men – and increasingly women – came together to gossip about the latest religious controversy, a new novel, the recent elections or the celebrities of the day. There were pleasure gardens, in Lambeth,

Vauxhall and, later, Chelsea, where for a small entrance fee customers could stroll among statues, dance to an orchestra, enjoy a play or a firework display, or dine *al fresco,* all the while watching and being watched by society. And of course there were the shops, selling the latest in clothes, furniture and ornaments, their dazzling merchandise glitteringly laid out before high-tech plate glass windows. No one had ever known anything like it before.

Just as the wars with France tended to arouse mixed feelings of pride and fear, so did the economic, political and cultural changes transforming England. Patriots crowed over British prosperity and fast-expanding empire, and sung the praises of her matchless constitution and unrivalled prowess. ('Sung' is the right word here: the 1740s saw the emergence not just of *God Save the King* but of James Thompson's *Rule Britannia,* with its triumphantly militaristic words, as (unofficial) national anthems.) Yet these changes were also a source of great dismay and, indeed, generally provoked more dismay than satisfaction. Most Englishmen, although they might enjoy the dividends of wealth, worried about the way they were generated.

Early eighteenth-century England was beset by an almost hysterical sense of corruption and decline: the literature and journalism of the period sometimes reads like one long moral panic. Looking downwards, the educated public complained that the lower sort had never been so given over to crime and sin. The first half of the century saw the creation of a barrage of voluntary societies devoted to spreading the Gospel and its message of obedience, hard work and sobriety, as well as a flood of laws imposing ever-harsher penalties on crime. It was the situation higher up the social hierarchy, however, which most alarmed true patriots. Where they should have been setting a good example to their inferiors, Britain's ruling class had succumbed to Gallic values and foreign luxury.

To men of the 'country' persuasion – the roast beef-eating classes – foreign luxury appeared harmful in at least two ways. First, it threatened, quite simply, to bankrupt the country. France and Italy in general, and Paris in particular, had long been 'esteemed the centre of taste, magnificence, beauty and everything that is polite', with the result that fashion, furniture, music, art and architecture were imported from the Continent or copied from it.[10] England's upper classes remained, at least until the French Revolution, thoroughly enamoured of France and spent a great deal of their wealth on French goods and services. The best families generally employed a French valet, and a French dancing master – looked on as an expert not only in dance and deportment but also in manners – as well as a French cook. They decorated their stately homes with French paintings, porcelain and furniture and patronised German musicians and Italian opera. This was the period when the Grand Tour emerged as an important aristocratic rite of passage. Young noblemen, having spent a fortune on foreign coaches, lodgings, servants and mistresses, food and wine, typically returned home festooned with expensive antiquities and fashionable gifts.

France's position as Europe's fashion queen was a source of deep resentment to many patriotically minded English artists and writers, Hogarth, Fielding, Johnson and Garrick among them. The Royal Academy, the British Museum and Johnson's *Dictionary of the English Language* and, in Scotland, Chambers' *Encyclopaedia Britannica,* were all born, at least in part, from the desire to outdo France. The same phenomenon – Britain's taste for all things French – prompted the establishment of an array of less lofty associations aimed at promoting English manufacture and trade over their foreign, French rivals, including the Association of Anti-Gallicans, founded by a group of tradesmen in London during the Jacobite rising of 1745, and the Society for the Encouragement of Arts, Commerce and Manufactures in Great Britain, founded in 1754. The Anti-Gallicans, whose aim was 'to discourage by precept and example, the importation and consumption of French produce and manufactures, and to encourage, on the contrary, the produce and manufactures of Great Britain', soon spread to major provincial capitals and beyond.[11]

Patriots did not just worry about the economic impact of foreign luxury. They feared for its effects on the English character. England's liberty, or so the argument went, depended on the existence of frugal, manly and upright patriots, fiercely jealous of their liberties and sensitive to their responsibilities – on the yeomanry and gentlemen of old. Yet this type was fast disappearing, as the English gave themselves over to the pursuit of place, to speculation and gambling, to Italian opera and French opulence. Seeking to explain Britain's catastrophic losses in the early years of the Seven Years War, the preacher John Brown had no hesitation in placing the blame on 'the luxurious and effeminate Manners' of those 'who are called the better sort'.[12] Schooled to believe that Israel had been undermined by venality, that Rome had been corrupted by Asiatic luxury, that ancient Britain had been occupied by an invading army of Norman aristocrats – committed to a mindset that said that only a nation of the most upright valour and virtue could hope to earn God's blessing – it seemed only too apparent that England was heading for ruin.

Once again, London, or at least its West End, was identified as the font of what Brown called 'Town-Effeminacy'. To most rural gentlemen and provincial traders the capital was a malignant growth; a place where courtiers and placemen, pimps and fops, pastry cooks and hairdressers united to drain the country of its wealth. Novels, journals and paintings depicted London, or more particularly, its western half, as a pit of corruption, a snare for innocent country folk, especially country girls, whom it sucked up, defiled and then spat out. But it was not only country dwellers who thought of the West End in this way. Just as fashionable society mocked the old City to the east, so the smaller merchants and tradesmen, 'the Cits', who dwelt there, derided the Whig magnates, fashionable foreigners and rich financiers who lived to the west. A moral geography was superimposed on to the architecture of the town.

One London figure in particular emerged in the late Stuart and early Georgian period as a focus of patriotic fears – the aristocratic fop, or beau, a snobbish mincing little thing, as smooth and rich as a French pâté. The French man of fashion and his West End follower, with their super-refined manners and extravagant dress, did in fact often go out of their way to bring attention to themselves – all the more so because, as Henri Misson observed, 'generally speaking, the English-men dress in a plain uniform manner'. Nevertheless, the fop quickly developed into a stock character of eighteenth-century art in a way that increased feelings against him. He first evolved in the theatre, making an early appearance with Etheredge's *The Man of Mode* of 1676, as Sir Flopping Flutter, 'lately arrived piping hot from Paris', complete with lisp, curled periwig and long gloves, and was refined to a cliché by the actor Colley Cibber in a series of roles stretching from around 1800 to 1830. As the Abbé Le Blanc explained to his French readers, Cibber was 'the most esteemed actor' of his generation: 'The part he excelled in was that of the French *petit-maître* and he made journeys to Paris to study their airs.'[13] Painters, print makers and novelists later took him up – no decent sized novel, in fact, was complete without him. The Frenchified fop and his counterpart, the forward, promiscuous, intellectual woman, represented the personification of everything the true patriot abhorred.

Hostility to European cuisine went back a long way. As early as 1547, Andrew Boorde was drawing a contrast between continental taste for insubstantial vegetables and English liking for good honest meat: 'Our English nature cannot live by roots, by water herbs or such beggary baggage.' At around the same time Sir Richard Morison wrote dismissively of Venice 'where frogges be a daintie disshe, snayles a morsel for a lady, where mushrumpes stand for a second course'. The Jacobean playwright Thomas Dekker derided 'kickshaws', a vulgarisation of *quelquechoses,* the light egg dishes beloved of French chefs.[14] Indeed, by the middle of the seventeenth century, the word 'kickshaw' had taken on a derogatory meaning, to describe any slight, vain or effeminate thing.

Patriotic moralists had, in particular, long objected to the English aristocracy's taste for foreign Catholic food. Already in 1577, William Harrison was referring disparagingly to the cooks of 'the nobility of England' who 'are for the most part musical headed Frenchmen and strangers'.[15] Writing in 1664, Robert May, author of *The Accomplisht Cook,* could complain that '*the French by their insinuations* . . . have bewitcht some of the *Gallants of our Nation* with Epigram Dishes, smoakt rather than drest, so strangely to captivate the *Gusto,* their mushroom'd Experiences for *Sauce* rather than *Diet,* for the generality howsoever called *A-la-mode,* not worthy of being taken notice on'.[16] (All this despite the fact that May was a Catholic who had trained in France and admitted to borrowing a number of recipes, particularly egg recipes, from La Varenne.)

The developments sketched in this chapter however – the threat of invasion from France or of French-backed, Catholic subversion from within, the decline in the standing and income of middle-class yeomen, squires, artisans and merchants and the neglect of old country ways, the corresponding concentration of power and money in a narrow ruling elite, and the upper class's treacherous preference for all things foreign – worked to turn a long standing disapproval of continental courtly food into a violent dislike. It is no coincidence that Campbell's indignant denunciation of French food was written in the immediate aftermath of the Jacobite uprising of '45 – Hogarth and Hanna Glasse (of whom more later) issued famously scorching indictments at around the same time.

Much like French and Italian patriots today, eighteenth-century Englishmen identified their national culinary traditions not just as one set of tastes and techniques among others, but as the encapsulation of home and hearth, Church and nation. It bound their world together. And like modern-day French and Italian patriots, early Englishmen naturally found in the threat to their culinary tradition a ready representation of larger, more elusive threats to all these ultimately important things. Substitute France for the United States, fricassees and wine for hamburgers and Coca-Cola and the parallels are striking. In a way that is not generally recognised, eighteenth-century England more or less kicked off modern kitchen nationalism.

5

Patriots in the Kitchen

> They fall into many contradictions regarding [the French]: they fear, and yet despise us; we are the nation they pay the greatest civilities to, and yet love the least; they condemn and yet imitate us; they adopt our manners by taste and blame them through policy.
>
> L'Abbé le Blanc, *Letters on the English and French Nations*, vol. I, 1747

SEVENTEENTH-CENTURY PATRIOTISM already included a good dose of food chauvinism, but it was only during the first half of the next century, as the fight against foreign corruption intensified, that it became a defining attribute of the loyal Englishman. This was the period when the individual voices raised against continental cooking swelled into a national chorus; when patriots began to celebrate the Elizabethan era as a time not merely of liberty and piety, but of good plain meat cookery; when Englishmen formed themselves into beef-eating clubs; when 'Beef and Liberty' became synonymous.

There were obvious reasons why patriots looked askance on the vogue for French cooking. It seemed outrageously wrong to many Englishmen to employ French chefs and to consume French-grown food and wine when Britain was at war with France – just as it was wrong to buy French furniture or fashion or employ a French valet. A

C.P. Boitard *The Imports of Great Britain from France*, 1757. This print showing the London docks was commissioned by the Association of Anti-Gallicans in an attempt to rouse patriotic sentiment against the fashionable worship of all things French. It is notable how many of the imports are culinary. In the middle of the crowd, just above the four porters on the lower left carrying a wooden case hung from two poles, several emaciated epicures welcome a French cook, 'acquainting him that without his Assistance they must have Perish'd with Hunger'. Frenchmen and connoisseurs of French food were always depicted as skinny – testimony both of the lack of nourishment and, more generally, the backwardness of the French economy. The three barrels on the lower right hand side, above crates of French perfume, millinery and muffs, contain claret, burgundy and champagne; next to them, a boy holds to nose to ward off the smell coming from an overturned barrel of Normandy cheeses. It was a telling reflection on the extent to which fine crafts were dominated by foreigners that even the anti-Gallicans had to employ one to make their print: Boitard was a Frenchman.

pound spent on a French chef or French wine was a pound denied to English cooks and native produce.

There were things to be said against French food, other than that it threatened to bankrupt the nation. To begin with, it was argued, it was snobbish.

Fricassees Are Snobbish

One set of publications perhaps did more than any other to launch English food chauvinism on its way.

The *Tatler* and its successor, the *Spectator,* were the work of two old school friends, Richard Steele and Joseph Addison, acquaintances of Swift and Pope, with well-established reputations as wits and writers on the London scene. The *Tatler,* which appeared three times weekly from 1709 to 1711, was Steele's creation, the *Spectator,* which came out every day until the end of 1712, was Addison's, but each man contributed to both papers and together they constituted two of the most influential works of literature ever to appear in England. The two journals were reprinted, in book form, dozens of times – the *Spectator*'s collected essays were republished more often than any other secular book in the eighteenth century. They had a profound influence on the way generations of Britons thought and behaved.

The *Tatler* professed to represent the 'lubrications' of Isaac Bickerstaff Esq, a learned gentleman whose high purpose and good sense were leavened by a mischievous wit. The *Spectator* gave voice to a 'Mr Spectator' and a 'club' of friends and correspondents. Both journals criticised the spirit of the religious and political factionalism that had dominated the seventeenth century, and preached a code of tolerance, politeness and innocent enjoyment in its place. Today both journals are generally remembered chiefly for their defence of commerce, their championing of arts and conversation – 'the pleasures of the imagination' – their quiet celebration of London coffee houses, clubs and diversions, and their moderate feminism. In all of this they set the standard for the ideal of politeness that proved vitally important to eighteenth-century English culture.

Despite their urbanity, however, the two publications were in many ways conventionally moralistic organs: Steele in particular showed a pronounced weakness for sermonising. They were against roughness, fanaticism and intolerance, but they were also against display, affectation and foreign influence. The gentle teasing tone that Bickerstaff adopted in the early issues gave way to something more earnest, as he took on 'the Title and Dignity of Censor of Great Britain' and set out 'to look into the Manners of the People and to Check any growing luxury, whether in *Diet,* Dress or Building' (emphasis added). He passed sentence not only on duels, bear baiting, forced marriages and the mistreatment of wives and daughters, but also on 'blue and red Stockings . . . tucked Cravats and Nightcap-Wigs', on snuff taking and canes hung from buttonholes – and overrefined, French food.

Addison and Steele returned to the campaign against French cooking on a number of occasions. One of their fictitious letter writers – 'one of those unfortunate men within the city-walls' who is married 'to a Woman of Quality' – complained about the fashionable dishes his wife served. 'I have a plain stomach, and have constant loathing of whatever comes to my own table, for which reason I dine at the chophouse three days a week . . . I am sure by your unprejudiced discourses you love Broth better than Soup.'[1] (The reference to soup serves as a reminder that it was not only the gravy/sauce distinction that separated the English from the French: the French also used their carefully created stocks to make mellifluous creamy soups.)

The brunt of their attack, however, was concentrated in one *Tatler* paper, written by Addison in 1710. Addison, or his spokesman Bickerstaff, begins by exhorting his readers to 'return to the Food of their Forefathers, and reconcile themselves to beef and mutton'.

> This was the Diet which bred that hearty Race of Mortals who won the Fields of Cressy and Agincourt. . . . The Renown'd King Arthur is generally looked upon as the first who ever sat down to a whole roasted Ox, (which was certainly the best way to preserve the Gravy) and it is further added, that he and his Knights sat about it at his Round Table, and usually consumed it to the very Bones before they would enter on any Debate of Moment. The Black Prince was a professed Lover of the Brisket; not to mention the History of the Sirloin [that is the story of its being ennobled by Henry VIII], or the Institution of the Order of Beef-Eaters, which are all so many evident and undeniable Marks of the great Respect which our War-like Predecessors have paid to this excellent Food. The Tables of the ancient Gentry of this Nation were covered thrice a Day with hot Roast-Beef; and I am credibly informed, by an Antiquary who has searched the Registers, in which the Bills of Fare of the Court are recorded, that instead of Tea and Bread and Butter, which has prevailed of Late Years, the Maides of Honour in Queen *Elizabeth*'s Time were allowed Three Rumps of Beef for their Breakfast.[2]

This defence of roast beef serves as prelude to an attack on the sort of fashionable dishes that had come to dominate London tables. Here Bickerstaff itemises exactly what he objects to in this form of cooking.

> Without expecting the Return of Hunger, they eat for an Appetite, and prepare Dishes not to allay, but to excite it.

> They admit of nothing at Their Tables in its natural Form, or without some Disguise.
>
> They are to eat every Thing before it comes in Season, and to leave it off as soon as it is good to be eaten.
>
> They are not to approve any Thing that is agreeable to ordinary Palates; and nothing is to gratify their Senses, but what would offend those of their Inferiors.

In short, the *Tatler* is saying, the only appeal that French food possesses is snob appeal. Its ingredients are hard to find, its recipes hard to cook, and its merits hard to appreciate.

By way of illustration Bickerstaff goes on to describe a supper party given by a 'friend' the previous summer – 'a great Admirer of the *French* Cookery, who (as the Phrase is) *eats well*'. The meal included a larded turkey disguised as 'a roasted Porcupine', rabbit disguised as pheasant, and several 'hashes' (pâtés), as well as a pig that had been deliberately 'whipped to Death'. The *pièce de résistance,* however, was the dessert, an extraordinarily elaborate confection arranged so as to form a pretty winter scene.

> There were several Pyramids of Candy'd Sweetmeats, that hung like Icicles, with Fruits scattered up and down, and hid in an artificial kind of Frost. At the same Time there were great Quantities of Cream beaten up into a Snow, and near them little Plates of Sugar Plumbs, disposed like so many Heaps of Hail-stones, with a Multitude of Congelations in Jellies of various Colours.

Bickerstaff's fellow guests might have been impressed by this showy display of wealth and refinement. (Summer ices in eighteenth-century London, after all, were an expensive novelty – the equivalent, perhaps, of feeding one's guests sashimi flown in privately from Japan).[3] Bickerstaff, however, was not.

> As soon as this Show was over I took my Leave, that I might finish my Dinner at my own House: For as I in every Thing love what is simple and natural, so particularly in my Food; Two plain Dishes, with Two or Three good-natured, cheerful, ingenious Friends, would make me more pleased and vain, than all that Pomp and Luxury can bestow.

Addison's paean to roast beef and his assault on food snobbery were to be repeated by many of his imitators.

Fricassees Will Seriously Damage Your Health

French food was not just condemned for being snobbish, it was also widely held to be unhealthy. *Tatler*'s roast beef issue gave influential expression to this point of view. There, Addison/Bickerstaff, noting the way 'many great Families are sensibly fallen off from the Athletick Constitution of their Progenitors' put it all down to food:

> I may perhaps be thought extravagant in my Notion; but I must confess, I am apt to impute Dishonours that sometimes happen in great Families to the inflaming kind of Diet which is so much in Fashion. Many Dishes can excite Desire without giving Strength, and heat the Body without nourishing it. . . . I look upon a *French* Ragoust to be as pernicious to the Stomach as a Glass of Spirits; and when I have seen a young Lady swallow all the Instigations of high Soups, seasoned Sauces, and forced meats, I have wondered at the Despair or tedious Sighing of her Lovers.

The *Tatler*, however, was not alone in suggesting that the abandonment of old English eating habits was undermining the health and prosperity of the nation. This was a claim made more or less seriously throughout the century. No less an authority than the Duke of Marlborough, the man who had led Britain to victory at Blenheim, had affirmed 'No soldier can fight unless he is properly fed on beef and beer'. Campbell's objection to 'the contagion' of French cooking was based, at least in part, on the belief that it was 'calculated not to supply the want of Nature, but to oppress her Faculties, disturb her Operations, and load her with, till now, unheard of Maladies'.

One man went further, however, than any other in elaborating on the sort of claims made in the *Tatler* and developing them into a medical theory.

Dr George Cheyne was the most celebrated medical writer of his age. Born in Aberdeenshire in 1671, he trained at Edinburgh's rising medical school where he became convinced that medicine had to be made over in the light of the new Newtonian science. Moving to London in 1702, he developed a flourishing West End practice, and published a series of books applying Newtonian principles to 'the Human Machine'. Cheyne never really departed from this 'iatro-mechanist' conception, according to which 'obstructions' within the body's many pipes and channels were the main cause of illness.

Cheyne's early books, however, proved unsuccessful, and their failure seems to have contributed to a nervous collapse. Over the next three decades, Cheyne, a charmingly guileless, oddly simple soul, carried on a long running war against weight gain, alcoholism and depression – at times he weighed as much as 450 pounds. Having found that none of the conventional cures – opium, mercury, the Jesuit bark – worked, he developed a dietary approach, which he then proceeded to advocate in a series of books: *Observation on Gout* (1720), *Essay of Health and Long Life* (1725) and *The English Malady* (1733). These combined autobiographical confession, mechanistic science, sociological theory and moralising social criticism. High living among London's *beau monde* had been the cause, Cheyne divulged, of his obesity and unhappiness. By retiring from society, however, and adhering to strict 'milk and seed' diet – no meat, no spices, no spirits – he had found health and happiness. England seemed to be suffering from an epidemic of melancholia and Cheyne's diet books became bestsellers. His patients included leading writers, politicians and noblemen; his name pops up in novels, plays and prints of the period; he became an intimate of the novelist Samuel Richardson; Dr Johnson commended his books.[4]

Cheyne's basic ideas were fairly simple. He believed that the northern races were physiologically unsuited to a refined or luxurious way of life. The French and the Italians were built for city living – for socialising, theatre going and gourmandising – but Englishmen were not. Hence the high rates of gout, melancholia ('the English malady') and other illness among them. Overindulgence at the table was especially harmful and Cheyne insisted relentlessly on the dangers of rich and indigestible dishes and distilled liquors. He was suspicious of culinary 'invention' in general, and foreign food in particular, especially when used to stimulate an artificial appetite:

> The ingenious mixing and compounding of *Sauces* with foreign *spice* and provocatives, are contriv'd, not only to rouze a sickly Appetite to receive the unnatural Load, but to render a good one incapable of knowing when it has had enough. Since French cookery has been in such Repute in England, and has been improv'd from Spain, Italy, Turkey, and every other Country that has any thing remarkably delicious, high, or savoury in Food; Since *Eastern* pickles and Sauces have been brought to embellish our continual feasts, food has become a form not of nourishment but poison.[5]

'The great rule', Cheyne stressed, 'of eating and drinking for health is to adjust the Quality and Quantity of our food to our digestive Powers.'

In his own day, Cheyne's name was most commonly associated with the vegetarian 'milk and seed' diet that he had used to cure his own melancholia. Yet Cheyne himself stressed again and again that he was only suggesting the renunciation of meat in extreme cases, when all else had failed and the patient was nervously wasting away. Indeed, he cautioned that for most people a diet without meat would be too weakening and his general standard of moderation was hardly austere: two chicken wings and a leg were about right for dinner. What Cheyne wanted, simply, was a return to a simple, old-fashioned diet – good plain food in moderation. Roast meat but no sauces, fermented drinks like ale, but not fortified ones like port or sack, and a minimum of salt, 'acid' and 'sulphurs'. The 'diet and manner of living of the middling rank, who are but moderate and temperate in foods of the common and natural products of the country, to wit in animal foods plainly dress'd and liquors purified by fermentation only . . . is', as he put it, 'that intended by the author of nature for this climate and country'.[6] Cheyne was not exactly a representative patriot – he was Scottish, after all. Nevertheless, in warning against the perils of eating foreign food, he spoke for all true Englishmen.

Fricassees Will Make You Poor

English critics had always complained that French cooking was expensive and wasteful. But the accusations now intensified, and for reasons that are not hard to see.

French cooking, it has been said, underwent something of a revolution in the 1720s and 1730s, as old-style court cuisine gave way to smaller, richer, ever more intense dishes, offering a single dominant flavour. On the face of it, English moralists might have been expected to welcome this move towards lighter, smaller dishes. Yet paradoxically, the new cuisine was more labour-intensive and expensive than the old. It relied on rich and costly *coulis* (meat glazes), prodigious quantities of cream, eggs, truffles, wine, and sugar, and rare and exotic garnishes. This was still luxurious cooking, only now it was subtly luxurious – and, as all true moralists know, subtle luxury is the most vicious luxury of all.

The charges of extravagance came from every quarter (they are implicit, for instance, in Addison's 1710 *Tatler* attack and the tirade in Campbell's *The London Tradesman*), but some of the loudest came from England's small army of women cookery writers. This again, is hardly surprising: they, or the housewife class for whom they spoke, were traditionally responsible for managing the family budgets and so were particularly sensitive to considerations of cost; perhaps they also felt a professional sexual rivalry with the highly paid male French chefs stealing their jobs and telling them how to cook. Contemporary newspaper advertisements show that a trained French chef (usually a man) earned anything from £20 to £60 per year. 'A good plain cook' (invariably a woman) earned from £6 to £10.[7]

One illustration will suffice. Hanna Glasse's *The Art of Cookery Made Plain and Easy*, published only two years after the Jacobite uprising of '45, in the middle of the War of Austrian Succession, was the best-selling English cookbook of the second half of the century, going into seventeen editions between its first appearance and 1803. One can see why. Glasse was the first in that long line of writers, stretching through Eliza Acton and Mrs Beeton to Delia Smith and Nigella Lawson, to take the housewife by the hand and reassure her that she understood her problems and her worries, that she shared her world. She addressed herself directly to the lady of the household and her cook, knowingly alluded to the difficulties posed by managing the male head of house – oh, so impractical, so status-conscious! – and offered them relatively detailed instruction for practical and affordable dishes. (Thus, at a time when cookery books were generally vague and obscure, Glasse made a point of using English rather than foreign words – 'pieces of bacon' for *lardons*; of suggesting substitutes for expensive or unobtainable ingredients, and of giving, at least by eighteenth-century standards, fairly precise quantities.) Just as important perhaps, Glasse was one of the first cookery writers to labour the virtues of domesticity and simplicity, and she did so precisely by defining her own approach in opposition to the French aristocratic tradition. So despite the fact that Glasse borrowed freely from French cookbooks, she also, like May, went out of her way to insult French chefs:

> If Gentlemen will have French Cooks, they must pay for *French* tricks. A *Frenchman*, in his own Country, would dress a fine Dinner of twenty Dishes, and all genteel and pretty, for the Expence he will put an *English* Lord to for the dressing of one Dish. . . . I have heard of a Cook that used six Pounds of Butter to fry twelve Eggs, when every Body knows, that Understands Cooking, that Half a Pound is full enough, or more than need to be used; But then it would not be *French*. So much is the blind Folly of this Age, that they would rather be imposed on by a French Booby, than give Encouragement to a good English Cook.[8]

The Art of Cookery Made Plain and Easy, indeed, has a whole chapter warning its readers off wasteful French sauces – 'Chapter III. Read this Chapter, and you will find how expensive a French Cook's Sauce is' – citing as typical a recipe for a brace of wild birds which involved, apart from the birds themselves, a roast partridge, the pinions (wings) of four turkeys, a quart of gravy, truffles, burgundy, onion, garlic, and thick ham stock. You might as well, Glasse tutted, 'boil a Leg of Mutton in Champaign'.

Ministers Like Fricassees

If the subtle extravagance of *nouvelle cuisine* was one factor that animated popular hostility to French food, and its unhealthiness another, a third was its popularity with England's ruling political elite – with the very people corrupting the country's ancient constitution, bankrupting its citizens and undermining its free manners. The Whig grandees' penchant for French food gave their enemies a perfect weapon.

Walpole, the most talented and powerful of the great Whig oligarchs, was naturally singled out for attack. Though he liked to play the gruff rustic squire, his opponents insisted that this was all a front; in fact Walpole was, they claimed, a corrupt and avaricious despot, set on milking the nation for all it was worth. He certainly had expensive tastes. From 1720 onwards the Prime Minister transformed his family's modest rambling Elizabethan house, Houghton Hall in Norfolk, into a magnificent Palladian stately home, transplanting a local village in the process. He built up one of the greatest art collections of the eighteenth century and one of the greatest cellars, spending recklessly on the best claret – Lafite, Latour, Haut-Brion – old burgundy, hock and champagne. His kitchens were, naturally, directed by a French chef, one Solomon Sollis, who had entered his service back in 1714 and later, as Walpole rose in power, provided an easy butt for his ever-increasing army of enemies.[9]

Walpole was in the habit of retiring to Norfolk once or twice a year, and the large parties he laid on for his friends and cronies there were viewed with special suspicion, as occasions for the hatching of all sorts of dubious deals and the consuming of all sorts of unnatural dishes. A representative opposition pamphlet of 1728, *The Norfolk Congress,* offered a mock-admiring account of one of Walpole's country banquets, which, it claimed, outdid even those laid on by Cardinal Wolsey, Henry VIII's notoriously ambitious and greedy chief minister. Much, in particular, was made of the foreign character of the food served – the Westphalian bacon, Dutch herring, French truffles, Spanish Ollio, the suspicious sounding *ambigu* – and the chef's very Catholic weakness for turning ordinary dishes into symbols. One dish, above all, stood out: 'an *English Collar of Brawn* stuck with *French Lillies,* instead of Rosemary'.

> At this many were offended, and said the times were hugely changed with our *Landlord* [Walpole], and his *Taste,* and *way of Living* strangely alter'd; for they remember'd when he had like to have overturned the whole Table, upon seeing some French Kickshaws upon it, which he would have said was poison to an *English Constitution.* But now, forsooth, nothing but *French Sauces* will go down . . .[10]

Walpole's close ally and successor, the Duke of Newcastle, opened himself up to similar criticism. Like Walpole, Newcastle grew unimaginably rich while in government. His palatial Surrey home, Claremont, was designed by Sir John Vanbrugh, with gardens laid out by William Kent. And while Walpole appears to have been more interested in furniture, painting and wine than food, Newcastle was a devoted and fashion-conscious gourmet – he was reputed to own one of the five solid gold dinner services in all of Europe. Early in the 1740s, notwithstanding the fact that Britain was at war with France, Newcastle managed to secure the services of Pierre Cloué, or Clouet, a leading exponent of *nouvelle cuisine,* a man whose 'light dishes and clear sauces' seduced all of fashionable London.[11] At some point in the late 1740s or early 1750s Cloué left London to return to Paris, where he became *maître d'hôtel* to Lord Albermarle, the British Ambassador and another great gourmet. Letters between Newcastle and Albemarle, and between Newcastle and Cloué himself, supply a comic record of Newcastle's desperate efforts to secure a replacement equally expert in *la cuisine qui est présentement à la mode dans les meilleures maisons de France* (when treating of food, Newcastle and Albermarle naturally wrote in French). After sacking the first chef sent over by Albermarle on the grounds that his 'soups are generally too strong, and his *entrées* and *entrements*' overly fussy ('it is impossible to guess what they are made of'), Newcastle, who was now Prime Minister, returned

Anon. *The Duke of Newcastle and his Cook*, 1745. It is hard to believe that Cloué would have had much use for the roasting jack shown in the print.

to the search, desperately worried that he would never be able to compete with Lord Monfort, whose cook, M. La Grange, was the toast of London: 'This town swarms with Frenchmen and there is scarce a young boy or even a country gentleman, who has not his French cook. Be so good as to do this for me; let me have a man of reputation who has served *dans les grandes maisons*'.[12] The correspondence ends happily, with Newcastle finally securing a chef called Fontenelle, a '*bon et grand cuisinier*' – although one, characteristically, a little too full of himself.[13]

Newcastle's penchant for snobbish and wasteful French chefs was naturally cause for much patriotic censure, with Cloué's extravagance in particular singled out for attack – it was said that he had once used twenty-two partridges to make a sauce for a couple of pigeons. A satirical print from the end of 1745, for instance, the high point of the Jacobite risings, shows Newcastle and his cook in their kitchen. The background to the print is provided by a government proclamation threatening enforcement of Elizabethan and Jacobean anti-Catholic laws that would have sent Cloué, a Catholic, back to France. The Duke, dismayed, exclaims, 'O! Cloe if you leave me, I shall be starv'd, by G-d!' The bill of fare draped over the kitchen table includes 'Woodcock's Brains', 'Carps Tongues' and 'Pope's Eye's.' These dishes, made up of absurdly small anatomical parts ('a pope's eye' was a small, tender nugget from the middle of a leg of mutton) are emblematic of the precious and insubstantial nature of fashionable French cuisine.[14]

6

Actors

Renown'd Sir-Loin, *oft times decreed*
The theme of English Ballad,
E'en Kings on thee have deign'd to feed,
Unknown to Frenchman's palate;
Then how much more they Taste exceeds
Soup-meagre, Frogs and Sallads.

From *The Roast Beef of Old England, A Cantata,* by Theodosius Forrest, as performed at the Haymarket Theatre, London, 1759

TO TRUE PATRIOTS, the invasion of foreign taste threatened to debase every corner of English life, including every corner of English cultural life. The contagion seemed all but unstoppable. The stage, or so the patriots argued, was a case in point. England's proud native dramatic tradition – the tradition of Shakespeare, and Johnson, Dryden and Congreve – had all but suffocated under a deluge of fashionable entertainments. The theatre – in Georgian England an enormously popular and influential cultural force – had become corrupted. It fell to a small band of playwrights, managers and actors to stand up for serious, manly English theatre – and to champion the virtues of roast beef.

If you had asked a patriotic critic of the mid-eighteenth century to pinpoint the beginning of the decline in the English stage, he would almost certainly have pointed to the arrival of Italian opera in the first decade of the century. The first full Italian opera, *Arsinoe, Queen of Cyprus*, had been performed in 1706, but opera really took off with the arrival of Handel in England in 1710 and the performance of his *Rinaldo*, the first London performance sung entirely in Italian, in 1711. From this point on, the Queen's Theatre, Haymarket, stopped offering spoken plays and devoted itself more or less entirely to foreign language operas.

The form proved immensely popular with the London crowds, who then, as now, liked a good musical, especially when it was spectacularly staged – Act I of *Rinaldo* calls for the heroine to be carried through the air in a 'Chariot drawn by two huge Dragons, out of whose Mouths issue Fire and Smoke', while Act II requires waterfalls, 'Thunder, Lightning, and amazing Noises'. The leading Italian singers were the pop idols of the day. Dazzlingly well paid, they attracted enormous publicity and an almost tribal loyalty.

Notwithstanding opera's popularity with people of quality, however, high-minded, patriotic Englishmen disapproved. The *Spectator* and *Tatler* inveighed against the new form and in defence of the 'manly Entertainments and Rational pleasures' of England's native theatre. Swift derided opera as 'unnatural' and 'wholly unsuitable to our northern climate, and the genius of the people, whereby we are overrun with Italian effeminacy and Italian nonsense'; Pope mocked it in *The Dunciad*; and Dr Johnson famously described it as 'an exotick and irrational entertainment, which has been always combated, and always prevailed'.[1]

To the critics, however, opera was only the most obvious manifestation of a more general corruption infecting England's stage. They disapproved of the all-night masquerades or fancy dress masked balls that Handel's Swiss collaborator John James Heidegger laid on at the Haymarket Theatre. They disliked the way theatre managers increasingly favoured a 'multiple bill' of musical performances, dance, acrobatics and light one-act comedies, over the traditional five-act play. And they deplored the fashion for pantomime, a strange mixture of mime, dance and song, usually based on some mythological story and often featuring the two *commedia dell'arte* characters, Harlequin and Columbine, that became fashionable in the 1720s.[2]

Despite the jeremiads, London's playhouses were not entirely given over to Italian operas and other lightweight tosh. Patriotism sometimes made itself heard. Foreign travellers indeed, often cited the London theatre as one domain where English 'freedom' revealed itself with particular expressiveness – or, as one put it, a little more critically, 'it is upon the stage chiefly, that English Liberty has degenerated into licentiousness'.[3] The irreverence of playwrights, actors and audience was a matter of touristic wonder.

This was true for much of the century: Guy Fawkes Day was celebrated with raucous performances of Nicholas Rowe's patriotic tragedy *Tamberlane*, an inspiring lesson in the duty of standing up to tyrants and despots. The overrefined, emancipated, clog-wearing ragout-eating French monsieur and the Frenchified English fop could always be relied upon to raise a laugh. But it was particularly true of the 1730s, when London's theatre became an important mouthpiece for popular opposition to Walpole and the court. This decade saw a remarkable flowering of vital, daring political theatre, a flowering that began with the spectacular success of John Gay's *The Beggar's Opera* of 1728, a biting satire on greed and government corruption, and ended when Walpole successfully passed the Licensing Act of 1737, effectively giving the state control over the theatres. In the interval, a series of anti-government farces and ballad operas inspired by Gay's *The Beggar's Opera*, many by Henry Fielding, dominated the stage.

It would be extraordinary if London's populist, sometimes raucous theatre had not become a vehicle for the expression of English food patriotism. In fact, it runs like a red thread through plays of the period. Two plays by the comic writer and actor Samuel Foote, for instance – *The Englishman in Paris* (1753) and *The Englishman Return'd From Paris* (1756) – which chart the magical transformation a young country buck into a slavish French fop after of a sojourn in Paris, make great play of young Buck's conversion from a taste for plain English cookery to French kickshaws; David Garrick, playwright and great Shakespearian actor, poked fun at the foppish appetite for tea; and Tobias Smollett's plays, like his novels, returned to mock French hunger and French food.[4]

Roast beef, in particular, had, by the middle of the century, established itself as a familiar stage symbol. The performance of an English translation of a French play, *The Frenchman in London*, in 1734, featuring a cartoon Englishman, Jack Roastbeef, a terse, no-nonsense merchant, direct to the point of rudeness, caused offence.[*5] But English playwrights were more than capable of replying in kind. In 1737 the French traveller L'Abbé Le Blanc attended the first play to be performed after the passing of Walpole's Licensing Act. The audience had arrived intent on booing the production off the stage in protest at the act, which was widely seen to trespass on ancient English liberties. The author, however (Le Blanc does not name him or his play) cleverly deflected the audience's anger by appealing to its patriotism:

> There was a long criticism upon our [French] manners, our customs and above all, upon our cookery. The excellence and virtues of English beef

*As this suggests, English merchants and traders working in France had acquired the nickname *rosbifs* by the beginning of the 1730s; by the end of the 1770s the moniker was being used to describe the English as a whole.

> were cried up, and the author maintain'd, that it was owing to the qualities of its juice that the English were so courageous, and had such a solidity of understanding, which rais't them above all the nations in Europe; he preferred the noble old English pudding beyond all the finest ragouts that were ever invented by the greatest geniuses that France has produced; and all these ingenious strokes were loudly clapp'd.[6]

If most of the playwrights of the day pandered to their audience's nationalism, one in particular left an enduring legacy to the roast beef cult. Henry Fielding, born in 1707, is now generally remembered as the author of two great novels: *Joseph Andrews* and *Tom Jones*. He also has a significant place in his country's political history, as a moral campaigner and reform-minded London magistrate. He began his career, however, as a playwright – the most successful of his day.

A gifted classicist, and a great admirer of Cervantes and Molière, Fielding was no crude chauvinist. Rather, he was an English cultural patriot of a recognisable kind: hostile to the conceited cosmopolitanism of the cultural elite, wary of aristocratic or royal patronage and determined to forge a new middle-class art of a characteristically English nature. He was, however, at least at this early stage in his career, willing to cater to his compatriots' more xenophobic prejudices. So his earliest poem, *The Masquerade,* and his first play, *Love in Several Masques,* both satirised Italian opera and Italianate masquerades; his later plays abound in affected French pantomime artists, absurd Italian singers, wicked Catholic confessors and other stock foreigners of the day.[7]

This, then, was the background to Fielding's contribution to English food bigotry. Around 1731, early in his career, he wrote a full five-act comic ballad-opera, *The Grub-Street Opera,* a satire on Walpole and the royal court. The play revolves around two contrasting families, that of the drunken, idle, tobacco addict, Squire Owen Apshinken (George II) and that of Mr Apshones, a tenant on his estate, a plain-speaking, upright countryman who dislikes the contagion of foreign fashions spreading outwards from London. ('Why', as he asserts at one point, 'have our women freshe complexions and more health in their countenances here than in London but because we have fewer beaux among us.') Sir Owen is merely idle but his family are more venal. His butler Robin (Walpole) is corrupt, embezzling family funds, while his son, Master Owen (the Prince of Wales), is a vicious fop, set on seducing Mr Apshones' virtuous daughter Molly. In this way the play draws a contrast between the corruption of the court and the virtue of the country it exploits. In a ridiculously unlikely denouement, Sir Owen falls in love with Molly, suffers a moral conversion and marries her.

In a scene towards the end of the play, Lady Apshinken (Queen Caroline, George II's wife), a dominating bully, runs through the day's bill of fare with Sarah, her cook. Sir Owen has invited some of his tenants to lunch in an act of 'old English hospitality'. Lady Apshinken, though, disapproves of wasting money on people of no importance and instructs the cook to serve only half the sirloin and hold back a partridge and the quince and apple pie. Susan protests – 'I wish I had been born in an age when there was some business for one! Before we had learnt this French politeness and been taught to dress our meat by nations that have no meat to dress' – and then bursts into song:

When mighty roast beef was the Englishman's food,
It ennobled our hearts, and enriched our blood,
Our soldiers were brave,
Our courtiers were good

Oh the roast beef of England
And old England's roast beef!

But since we have learnt from all conquering France
To eat their ragouts as well as to dance,
Oh what a fine figure we make in romance!
Oh the roast beef of England
And old England's roast beef!

Then, Britons, from all nice dainties refrain,
Which effeminate Italy, France, and Spain
And mighty roast beef shall command on the main
Oh the roast beef of England
And Old England's roast beef!

As it turned out, *The Grub-Street Opera* was never performed – Fielding suppressed it after being bribed, or perhaps threatened, by Walpole. But the playwright found another chance to air his splendidly patriotic song (sung to the tune of a well-known air, *The Queen's Old Courtier*) three years later, when he bolted it on to another ballad opera, *Don Quixote in England,* a satire on the corrupt electoral politics of a country borough. This *was* performed, in 1734. Fielding's ballad – a contribution to a long standing tradition of eating and drinking songs – proved a great hit. During the next few years Richard Leveridge, another playwright and songwriter and author of yet another burlesque on Italian opera, gave it five new stanzas and set it to another, catchier tune.[8] In this version, *The Roast Beef of Old England* remained a favourite well into the nineteenth century and was, itself, often adapted. It was sung on patriotic occasions, feasts and festivals, and, of course, in the theatre, where it was chanted in the galleries between acts but also employed to accost any foppish characters or foreign performers who appeared on the stage.

At a time when song was much more important than it is today – when dinners ended in song and work, travel and merrymaking were accompanied by it – Fielding had given the English a culinary national anthem.

London audiences, then, were used to hearing roast beef's praises sung on stage. But actors did not just commend beef in public. They also formed clubs devoted to celebrating it behind the scenes.

The earliest of these seems to date from the first years of the eighteenth century. Hardly anything is known about this first 'Beef-Steak Clubb', although in its time it was a prestigious affair, gathering prominent gentlemen, actors and writers, at least some of whom had close connections to one of London's principal theatres, Drury Lane. These included Richard Estcourt, a well-known actor and mimic, and possibly Richard Steele, who, as well as writing for the *Tatler* and the *Spectator*, had created comedies and tragedies for Drury Lane. Richard Estcourt was a famously funny and gregarious soul – Steele described him as 'the best man that I know of for heightening the revel-gaiety of a company' – and seems to have been the spoke around which the club revolved. As 'Providore', or host, he would have organised the club's meetings and overseen the grilling of the steaks eaten at every gathering. Estcourt also kept a small book in which the sayings, jokes and stories of club members were entered. In return, he got to wear the club badge, a small gold gridiron or grill, 'hung about the neck on a green Silk Ribbon'.[9]

By the 1750s, Dublin and Cambridge, among other cities, had their own 'beefsteake' theatre clubs, where writers, actors and patrons gathered to eat steaks, sing jocular patriotic songs, and swap stories –

the Dublin one was founded in 1753 by Thomas Sheridan, father of the playwright Richard Brinsley Sheridan, and manager of the Theatre Royal. Unusually the presidency was held by a woman, Peg Woffington, Ireland's most famous actress.[10]

The most significant, long lasting and best documented of these clubs, however, was the Sublime Society of Beefsteaks, set up in London in 1736. Its three founding members appear to have been John Rich, George Lambert and William Hogarth. Rich was one of the two or three top theatrical figures of his day, producer of *The Beggar's Opera*, manager of Covent Garden Theatre and an acclaimed pantomime actor. Lambert, only twenty-five, was Rich's senior scene painter at the Covent Garden, as well as an established landscape artist – he had supported Hogarth's successful campaign, earlier in the year, to secure copyright for artists in their own works, an important achievement that much improved the standing of British artists. Hogarth, in turn, in his mid-thirties and a rising star, had long been inspired by the stage, had many theatrical friends, and often painted actors and theatrical scenes, including Gay's *The Beggar's Opera*.

Accounts of the club's origins differ. According to one tradition, George Lambert, not having time for a regular dinner, 'contented himself with a beef steak broiled upon the fire in the painting room' – a room behind the stage. Sometimes visitors joined him and by and by the Beefsteak Club was born. Another story has Rich in place of Lambert. Either way, the Beefsteaks met in a large room above the theatre, which slowly took on the character of a club, as drawings, paintings and other paraphernalia given by members spread over its walls.[11]

At first it seems a little surprising to see Rich, whose name was indelibly linked to pantomime, so closely associated with the Beefsteaks. Patriotic critics, after all, liked to blame him for the corruption of the

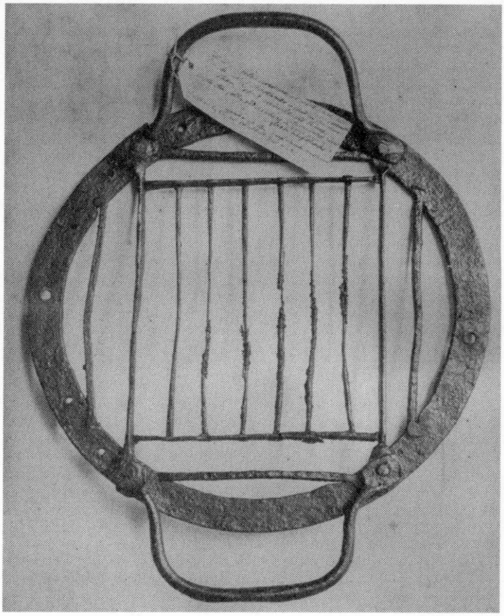

The Beefsteak Club gridiron

English stage. Pope mocked him in *The Dunciad*, singling out his reliance on expensive scenery and elaborate stage effects:

Immortal Rich! how calm he sits at ease,
Mid snows of paper and fierce hail of pease,
And proud his mistress' orders to perform
Rides in the Whirlwind and directs the Storm.

Fielding lampooned him in a number of plays. Even Hogarth, now his associate, had satirised one of his pantomimes, *Harlequin and Dr Faustus*, in an early print, *The Taste of the Town*. Perhaps Rich defended his productions with the claim that he was only catering to public taste;

or perhaps he argued, with his fellow pantomime artist John Weaver, that while Italian and French pantomime was corrupt and debauched, the English version had some of the rigour and purity of its ancient originals – that pantomime, while not rising to the heights of spoken tragedy and comedy, was well adapted to the edification of a people 'sunk into Effeminacy'.[12]

However Rich justified his work, there is no doubt that the Beefsteak Society was a patriotic, anti-French association. Fielding himself was never a member, but *The Roast Beef of Old England* was sung at every meeting until the 1760s, when a new member, Theodosius Forrest, composed a special club song, *The Song of the Day,* which was every bit as patriotic:

No more shall Fame expand her wings
To sound of heroes, states, and kings;
A nobler flight the Goddess takes,
To praise our British Beef in steaks,
A joyful theme for Britons free,
Happy in Beef and Liberty.

Throughout the realms where despots reign,
What tracks of glory now remain!
Their people, slaves of power and pride,
Fat Beef and Freedom are denied!
What realm, what state, can happy be,
Wanting our Beef and Liberty?

Indeed, the club's very name, the Sublime Society of Beefsteaks, worked, like Gay's *Beggar's Opera* or Fielding's *Grub-Street Opera,* as a dig at continental, aristocratic pretensions. French theorists tended to the view that art should avoid the everyday and focus on the sublime; Fielding, Hogarth and their friends took a more down-to-earth position.

Membership of the Beefsteaks was limited to twenty-four. In the original roll of members, five describe themselves as 'comedians' or actors, but the majority, including two well-known dancers, had connections with the theatre. In time the club developed strong aristocratic and even royal associations: the Prince of Wales, later George IV, joined in the 1780s, followed by his brothers. But only one of its original members possessed a title – and he was only a baronet. The rest were prominent well-to-do citizen patriots of middling, yeoman rank – your quintessential, patriotic 'Freeborn Englishmen'. They included, in addition to the actors, dancers and painters, a lawyer, doctor, owner of a coffee house, stonemason and sculptor, silversmith, lacemaker, three merchants, and the Warden of the Fleet Prison.

The Beefsteaks met every Saturday during the theatrical season, from October to June. Members were expected to attend most gatherings or resign. Beef was the only meat ever served, eaten, of course, with mustard or horseradish, and other plain, manly accompaniments like baked potatoes, onions, beetroots and toasted cheese. These were washed down with generous quantities of porter, port, punch and whisky toddy. Grilling of the steaks began at two in the afternoon and tablecloths were removed at three-thirty.

Like many clubs of the era – and this was the great age of the club, with thousands in London alone – the Sublime Society of Beefsteaks sought to bind its members together through ceremony and ritual. The Beefsteaks, indeed, had a particularly elaborate set of rites, echoing those of the fast-expanding Freemasons. Like so much about the club, these seem to have been executed in a spirit that was half-satirical and half-serious. Club members sported the badge of

The Beefsteak Club medal

the society, a silver medal stamped with a gridiron, and bearing the club's motto, 'Beef and Liberty'. (This clearly looked back to the earlier medal worn by Estcourt.) Later, other regalia were created, including rings, cutlery and tankards, all, again, stamped with the club's symbol and motto. For a period 'Beefsteaks' even had a uniform – blue coat and waistcoat, with brass buttons, bearing, once again, the words 'Beef and Liberty'.

Club members took it in turns to play its 'officers': President, Vice President, Bishop, Recorder and Boots. The 'President' of the day sat under a canopy, with a Beefeater's hat and plume hanging on the back of his chair. He was obliged to sing, 'whether he could or not', one of the club's official beef anthems, propose toasts, and read out any resolutions. 'Boots', always the newest member, had to serve as the 'fag of the brotherhood', bringing the steaks individually from the spit to the diner and pouring the wine. The 'Bishop', dressed in full ecclesiastical regalia, and accompanied by 'halberdiers' in absurd costumes, no doubt ransacked from the costume room of the theatre, had to bring in new members, blindfold, and make them swear and kiss a book – for which a bone of beef was substituted. Practical jokes were plotted, lewd songs recited and outrageous toasts encouraged – and all were sworn not to repeat them outside the meeting.[13] Boswell, who spent a drunken evening at the Beefsteaks in 1762, recorded that 'We had nothing to eat but beefsteak, and had wine and punch in plenty and freedom. We had a number of songs.'

The President on that occasion, Boswell noted, was Lord Sandwich, a close associate of the leading radical patriot, John Wilkes, the most outspoken opposition figure of his day, and himself a member of the club.[14] By this stage, indeed, the club had a well-established reputation as a stronghold of unaffected native virtue. An issue of the London weekly, *The Connoisseur,* lamenting the eclipse of old English cooking by a Frenchified diet of 'high soups and rich sauces', singled out the Beefsteaks for praise:

> Our only hopes are in the Clergy, and in the Beef-steak Club. The former still preserve, and probably will preserve, the rectitude of their appetites; and will do justice to Beef, wherever they find it. The latter, who are composed of the most ingenious artists in the kingdom, meet every Saturday in a noble room at the top of Covent-Garden theatre, and never suffer any dish except Beef-steaks to appear. These, indeed, are most glorious examples; but what alas! Are the weak endeavours of a few to oppose the daily inroads of fricassees and soup-maigres! This . . . is a national concern, as it may prove more destructive to Beef than the distemper among the horned cattle; and should the modish aversion

against rumps and sirloins continue, it will be absolutely necessary to enforce the love of Beef by act of parliament.[15]

The Sublime Society of Beefsteaks continued to meet on a weekly basis in Covent Garden until that theatre burnt down in 1808, when it moved to the Bedford coffee house, a meeting place for actors and playwrights, and then to another theatre, the Old Lyceum, before ending up in a specially built suite of rooms in the roof of the New Lyceum. The club folded in 1867, at which point its members included two earls, two baronets, and the future Prime Minister, William Gladstone. The strange rites and the copious consumption of good English beef were practised right until the end.

Not that this quite finished off the Sublime Society. A successor, the Beefsteak Club, was founded nine years later, and continues to this day as a gentlemen's club (no women members allowed) off Leicester Square. As in the past, the club occupies one large room, most of which is taken up by a communal dining table, and is busiest at lunchtime. It retains some of the club's original livery including cups, rings and furniture, bearing the club's motto and gridiron. It also continues the old tradition whereby all the club's servants, regardless of their names, are known as 'Charles'. Hogarth would be pleased to see the walls hung with an impressive collection of his works. The club is popular with patriotic Tory gentlemen – it held a special breakfast for country members attending the 2002 'Liberty and Livelihood' march in favour of fox-hunting. The view that contemporary Beefsteaks take of continental Europe, as a corrupt and dangerous place with worrying designs on Britain, would have rung bells with Rich, Lambert, Hogarth and their friends. Sadly, however, the club no longer has any association with the theatre. Worse, beefsteak is no longer the only dish served.

7

Hogarth

The Connoisseurs and I are at war.
William Hogarth

WILLIAM HOGARTH, PUG-DOG small, cocksure and quarrelsome, is a central figure in this story. His life and work embody the spirit of eighteenth-century English nationalism, he co-founded the Sublime Society of Beefsteaks, and many of his art works, most famously *The Gate of Calais,* give expression to native food chauvinism. And because he was a great artist – perhaps the first great English artist – he deepened and enriched the themes this book is about.

Surprisingly little is known about Hogarth's life. Only one letter from him survives, while his unfinished autobiographical notes, like the observations of his contemporaries, are frequently distorted by the conflicts that raged around him. It is often hard, moreover, to make sense of the evidence that has survived, just as it is hard to make sense of Hogarth's rich and complex pictures. He could play the lout, shitting on graves or on the steps to a church; he liked scurrilous puns, bawdy songs and dirty drawings. But he aspired to the rank of gentleman, and married the daughter of Sir James Thornhill, the leading English painter of his age and Sergeant Painter to the king. Proud and defensive, he showed an extraordinary ability to antagonise potential friends and patrons, yet early in his career he also displayed considerable political skill in persuading Parliament to pass an Act giving artists copyright in their prints – it was known as 'Hogarth's Act'. He was a brazen self-publicist, but also a dedicated philanthropist and a proud and independently minded 'patriot', who in the end accepted a Court appointment. Above all, his paintings combine crude sloganeering with nuance, playfulness and great depth of feeling. He remains a bit of an enigma.[1]

Hogarth was born in 1697, in the vicinity of Smithfield, London's main cattle market, and remained through and through a Londoner. The city, with all its wretched, richly coloured goings-on, forms the backdrop to most of his pictures. As a young man, Hogarth's father had come from north-west England to the capital to seek his fortune. A teacher, translator and author of textbooks, he was enterprising and inventive but still unsuccessful – a failed Grub Street hack. His wife, Hogarth's mother, was reduced to selling quack medicines to keep the family together. Hogarth, then, grew up in straitened circumstances, in small dark houses and rank streets. His father died when his son was twenty but not before being confined to the Fleet Prison for debt. Hogarth himself put his death down to 'disappointments from great men's promises'.

Like his father, Hogarth was determined and resourceful, but he was also worldlier. 'Taken', as he put it, 'early from school', he served 'a long apprenticeship to a Silver plate engraver'. He found working as a jobbing engraver frustrating and demeaning, and soon began to create inventive works of his own, including political satires on two stock targets of the 1720s, the South Sea Bubble and the Lottery, and, a little later, *The Taste of the Town*, satirising the fashion for foreign masques, operas and light-hearted comedies. In his late twenties, he began to experiment with oils, learning to paint with marvellous speed. His paintings of *The Beggar's Opera* (1728–9) are memorable on many counts: for the fact that he depicted both audience and play; for their character as a painto-journalistic record of a contemporary event; for their daring satire on living politicians; but most of all for their bold and confident style. Over the next two or three years, Hogarth established a reputation as a painter of what he described as 'small family pieces and conversations', but it was two longer series of paintings of the early 1730s that made him famous: *A Harlot's Progress* and *A Rake's Progress.* The prints he made of them became bestsellers. For the first time, the general public could buy a serious work of art by an English artist.

The two series have much in common. Both follow the downward journey of young people undone by the metropolis. Moll Hackabout, an innocent country girl, arrives in town only to fall into the hands of an old prostitute turned procuress, who establishes Moll as mistress to a wealthy Jew. Before long she is reduced to working as a common whore, and then imprisoned and forced to beat hemp in Bridewell house of correction; the last two paintings depict her painful and squalid death from venereal disease. Where Moll is poor, Tom Rakewell, the 'hero' of *A Rake's Progress,* is heir to a rich father, whose death allows Tom to set himself up in the West End as a man of quality. Soon however, Tom, too, is in trouble, contracting the clap and being arrested for debt. In desperation, he marries a rich old hunchback, but rapidly loses her money on the gambling table, by which time he is already showing the first signs of syphilis-induced insanity. The last terrifying painting shows him dying in Bedlam, naked but for his chains, surrounded by madmen.

It is not just their story lines that they share. Both series work in the same way. Where English painters before Hogarth had been content to follow aristocratic, continental fashion, concentrating on portraits of their patrons or 'history paintings' of elevated epic and religious scenes, the 'progresses' represent a new sort of oxymoronic, high–low visual art (Hogarth christened them 'comic history paintings') that focused on the follies and vices of the contemporary world. Hogarth's creations are not simply comic: at their best they rise to great emotional heights. But with their clear modern stories, their depiction of real places and people, their puns and jibes and fierce patriotism, they spoke to England's ordinary people – the men of the taverns and coffee houses, the women of the markets and lending libraries – rather than traditional aristocratic connoisseurs. Hogarth's friend Henry Fielding called them 'novels in paint'. Artfully composed, with a painter's feel for order, hierarchy and colour, they nevertheless teem with action and incident, noises, tastes and smells, with signs, paintings, plays and books. They ask to be read.

As you would expect in works so rich, both 'progresses' connect in many ways with the patriotism that was so important to Hogarth. Moll's first client is a Jew; a Eucharist wafer (suggesting she has dabbled with Catholicism) can be seen near her bed; costumes for an Italian masque spill from a trunk in her room. Many of the milestones on Moll's road to ruin bear a foreign script.

But it is *The Rake's Progress* that gives most forthright expression to Hogarth's love of country. The central picture in this respect is the second, *The Rake's Levée*. This witty satire depicts the Rake, extravagantly dressed, newly established in his lavish West End quarters, playing host to a circle of hangers-on at his morning levee. Tom stands beneath some earlier purchases: an overblown *Judgement of Paris,* in the epic manner, and some absurd cocks in the 'low' Dutch style – a dig at the two extremes to which, Hogarth believed, most continental art tended.

The men clustered around Tom also represent two further extremes, between which Tom and Englishmen like him are pulled. The presence of a jockey and a prizefighter indicate his liking for hearty, mindless English country sports. But they have to compete for his attention, and his money, with purveyors of shallow European fashion: a composer of opera, complete with impossibly large cuffs, a French fencing teacher, and a tiny French dancing master, standing on tiptoes, with a ridiculously small viola in his hands. No doubt the rake had already employed a French chef.

The two moral progresses established Hogarth's fame, but they did not win his war. Hogarth deeply resented the way English art aped foreign fashion and hated being dependent on rich patrons. He wanted the creation in England of an independent and respected school of naturalistic painting, unaffected by what he saw as the pretentiousness and formality of European art. However, he faced disappointment and ridicule, and his lifelong opposition to an official academy of art – he believed that formal academies on the French model discouraged originality – came to nothing: by the time he died in 1764 the Royal Academy of Art was being set up.

Hogarth was canny enough to turn many of his setbacks to his advantage. An inspired propagandist, he cultivated a reputation for himself as a doughty fighter. He made a spectacle of his patriotism, publicly mocking the 'ship Loads of dead Christs, Holy families, Madonas and other dismal Dark Subjects', flogged to poor English collectors, by unscrupulous '*Picture-Jobbers from abroad*'. As head of the St Martin's Lane Academy, a relatively informal art school, offered as a self-conscious alternative to a French-style academy, he influenced a generation of students. Circumventing the picture dealers, he held his own well-publicised auctions and financed his own subscriptions. If Hogarth succeeded in this way in alienating many of the leading patrons of the day, he had his own following among younger painters, writers and actors, many of them great and influential in their own right, including Samuel Richardson, Fielding and David Garrick, who identified with his modern, naturalistic art and his elevated vision of the artist.

Hogarth, then, was a patriot, yet positive images of England are harder to find in the first half of his career than negative images of the foreigner and of foreign fashions. For all Hogarth's xenophobia, the moral progresses paint London as a terrible place. His scathing satire was unpartisan, a point clearly illustrated by the painting *Noon*, from Hogarth's series of 1738, *The Four Times of Day*, each of which records a different moment in the passing of the day. Like all the others in the series, *Noon* is set in Covent Garden. A gutter in the pavement separates two groups of people and divides the painting in two. On the one side, a procession of French worshippers leaves the Huguenot church, displaying either extreme sobriety or extreme foppishness – another dig at the failure of foreigners, or at least Frenchmen, to find a happy medium between extremes. But the figures on the English side of the painting are hardly depicted any more sympathetically. Like links in a chain, a black servant fondles the breasts of a serving maid who pours the contents of a pie over a howling baker's boy, who drops the lunch he is carrying on to the pavement, where it is filched by a street urchin.

If the French depicted in *Noon* embody the vices of order and artifice, the English personify those of greed and lust. In an intimation of Hogarth's later use of food imagery, the painting even gestures to

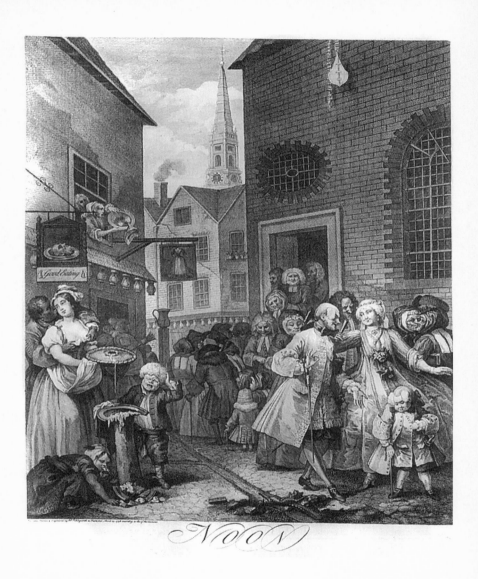

William Hogarth, *Noon*, 1738

the culinary dimension to the contrast between the two nations. The kite hanging limply from the Huguenot church looks suspiciously like a flatfish, and is mirrored by a leg of lamb being hurled out of a window on the English side of the picture. Just as meat was associated with England, fish, eaten by Catholics on Fridays and during Lent, was associated with France – poor, bony flatfish especially so. It is a witty, characteristically Hogarthian touch.

From the mid-1740s, however, emphatically positive depictions of England *do* begin to appear in Hogarth's art. The reason is not difficult to fathom. Britain and France had been at peace since 1713, but the War of Austrian Succession was to begin again in 1743, and with it the threat of French invasion and a barrage of anti-French propaganda. The stakes, already high, increased dramatically in the summer of 1745, when the Young Pretender, Prince Charles Edward Stuart, grandson to James II, landed in Scotland and gathered an irregular army. At first the threat was hardly taken seriously but complacency soon gave way to panic. In September 'Bonnie Prince Charlie' succeeded in defeating government forces at Prestonpans, east of Edinburgh. By the beginning of December the Jacobite army had advanced into England and taken Derby. In London, only a few days' march away, city merchants packed their belongings, ready to flee. At the last moment, however, the Prince decided to return north. At Culloden Moor, near Inverness, in April 1746 the much better equipped forces of the Duke of Cumberland, George II's young son, mercilessly slaughtered the Pretender's supporters.

The '45 and its aftermath elicited a veritable flood of patriotic propaganda – plays, verses, prints and broadsheets warned against the horrors to be anticipated from Stuart victory or celebrated its defeat. Yet Hogarth, perhaps preoccupied with a large commission for the Foundling Hospital, was uncharacteristically slow to respond to the crisis, publishing no print for as long as it lasted.* It was three years after the uprising that he finally turned to it, although now it became the subject of one of his greatest paintings. *The March to Finchley* depicts the December day in 1745 when London learnt that the rebels had reached Derby. All the regular regiments that might have been expected to defend the city were either fighting abroad or had moved north to put down the rebellion in its heartland, and the capital was unprotected. Three regiments of patriotic footguards, horse grenadiers and lifeguards, however, had been quickly assembled, and Hogarth's painting shows them saying their farewells at the Tottenham Court turnpike, before embarking to set up a defensive camp in Finchley, just north of the city.

As so often with Hogarth, the painting and the print he made of it are complex and allow different readings. Hogarth's subtly composed depiction of the ragged recruits, their friends and relatives, framed by sturdy English brick buildings and a gentle cloud-scattered sky, is far from uncritical. An imbecilic drummer on the left drowns out the din made by his wife and child; a soldier gropes a milkmaid

*The Foundling Hospital, essentially an orphanage, had been established in 1737. Hogarth, who sat on the board of governors, was closely associated with it from the beginning. As well as executing a large painting, he designed a uniform and coat of arms for the children, and presided over the annual meeting of artists that took place every 5 November in honour of the Revolution of 1688. A self-consciously modern English institution and the first philanthropic organisation to be run like a commercial company, the Hospital aimed to turn orphans into productive members of society; once grown, boys were to be sent to sea or to work in husbandry, girls to be employed as servants. It is not surprising then that the catering was typically English: during the week the foundlings were fed either boiled meat, suet pudding or gruel; on a Sunday they were given roast beef or in the pork season, roast pork. On the annual holiday that marked the foundation of the orphanage, and on other special occasions, they were again served roast beef, although this time with the luscious addition of plum pudding (see John Drummond and Anne Wilbraham, *The Englishman's Food*, p. 225).

William Hogarth, ***The March to Finchley*****, 1749**

while his mate empties one of her pails into his three-cornered hat. On the right, a soldier, lying in a puddle, turns away from a friend offering him water and reaches out to his wife for a swig of gin. Indeed, George II, who had the famous painting brought to him, was outraged at Hogarth's low portrayal of his soldiers. He 'probably expected', one contemporary recorded, 'to see an allegorical representation of an army of heroes devoting their lives to the service of the country; and their sovereign, habited like the mailed Mars on a cloud'.[2] Instead he was presented with a festival of folly and vice.

But although this is an undeceived view of England, it is also, ultimately, a patriotic one. We are in little doubt that the central figure, the grenadier, asked to choose between the pregnant hag on the right, with a Catholic cross around her neck, and the equally pregnant ballad seller on the left, with a copy of the Protestant Hanoverian anthem, *God Save the King*, hanging from the basket, will choose the latter. In just the same way, we know that the crowd of grotesques to the fore will become the ordered troops marching off in the background. It might be better, Hogarth seems to be saying, if the English were less lustful, drunken and violent than they are, but they can at least be relied upon to defend their freedoms and their country.

The patriotism of *The March to Finchley* was surpassed by that of another Hogarth painting of the same year, *The Gate of Calais*, which contributed very directly to English food chauvinism. In May 1748 the War of Austrian Succession finished, at last, in a compromise. With the continental ports open again, English tourists and connoisseurs flooded into France, Hogarth among them. For all his chauvinism, Hogarth had been to Paris before, in 1743, just before the outbreak of war, and had apparently enjoyed himself, returning with a feeling for the kind of paintings being done there and some sense of the popularity his engravings enjoyed. Now he set off again with a group of artist friends. According to one early biographer, Hogarth behaved appallingly, criticising everything he saw: 'If an elegant circumstance, either in furniture, or the ornaments of a room, was pointed out as deserving approbation, his narrow and constant reply was, "What then? But it is French! Their houses are all gilt and be[shi]t".' In the streets he was often outrageously rude. 'A tattered bag, or a pair of silk stockings, with holes in them, drew a torrent of imprudent language from him.' The source for this story is admittedly far from trustworthy but Hogarth himself, in an uncompleted account of the journey, gave vent to his prejudices: French life was 'a farcical pomp of war, parade of riligion, and Bustle with very little business [–] in short, poverty, slavery and Insolence . . .'.

Hogarth's friends must have been pleased to escape France without taking a beating, but their journey back to England was not without incident. Calais had been owned by the English as relatively recently as 1558 – it was the last of England's continental territories to go – and while waiting there for a boat, Hogarth set out to explore the town. As he would later explain, he 'was sa[u]ntering about and observing [the people] & the gate' to the old city, taking pride in the fact that it 'was built by the English when the place was in our possession (there is a fair appearance still of the arms of England upon it)'. Perhaps with a patriotic painting already in mind, he decided to make a sketch, but was quickly 'seized and carried before the Governor' – and charged with spying. After demonstrating that he was an artist and not a military engineer, allegedly by drawing withering caricatures of Frenchmen, he was placed under house arrest until his boat was ready to sail.

Back home, stories about the incident spread quickly, not all of them to Hogarth's credit. Some said that the famous artist had been abused and humiliated, others that he had provoked his arrest. Hogarth saw his chance. As soon as he was safe in England, he set to work on a painting that would appeal to every English patriot, while also making sure that he had the last word.

Hogarth was not the first graphic artist to draw on popular culinary prejudice. Already in the seventeenth century, popular artists had depicted the Dutch as living on fat, butter and pickled herring.[3] Later, with the outbreak of war at the end of the 1730s, patriotic print makers again represented the threat posed by the England's enemies, chiefly Spain and France, in terms of food – or rather its absence. *Slavery,* a print of 1738 criticising Walpole's failure to respond to Spanish aggression in the Caribbean, showed England enslaved by a Spanish tyrant, with English prisoners forced to eat roots and to pull a plough through barren soil.

The *Chevaliers Market,* created at the height of the Jacobite uprising of '45, foretold the terrible consequences of its success. A sturdy Englishman, reduced to slavery, sweeps away the Magna Carta and the Protestant Bible; the Protestant church has been turned into a Catholic temple offering indulgences and miracles; and market stalls sell fake holy relics, wooden clogs 'à la mode Paris', French brandy and 'fine plump frogs for a fricassee'.

The work Hogarth now created, however, was far richer and more complex than any of its predecessors; it was also the first, it seems, to feature roast beef.

One of Hogarth's masterpieces, *The Gate of Calais* is exquisitely detailed and beautifully coloured, full of cool greys and blues offset by dashes of red. At the same time it has about it the simple, bold

Anon., *The Chevaliers Market: or Highland Fair,* 1745

William Hogarth, *The Gate of Calais*, 1749, Tate Britain, London

quality of a modern poster – it would not look amiss on a billboard today. At the centre we see a thin kitchen porter, wearing *de rigueur* bagwig and stockings, straining under the weight of a vast, glistening joint of raw beef, destined for the English tourists staying at 'Madam Grandsire's', a local, English-owned hotel. The kitchen porter, in turn, is surrounded by a large cast of equally familiar characters: a gross monk greedily fondling, or perhaps blessing, the joint, two scrawny gormless soldiers, and a ragged *petit-maître*, his toes poking through his stockings, all transfixed by the sight of the meat. The scene is mirrored in the two cooks in wooden clogs carrying a large kettle of watery *soupe maigre*, the poor French answer to roast beef. In addition, a number of figures stand apart from this scene. In the right foreground, a poor tartan-clad Jacobite, a veteran of the '45, languishes against a wall, with an onion – his sole source of nourishment – beside him. To the left, three superstitious old hags, perhaps fishwives (they could also be nuns) huddle around a flatfish, pointing in superstitious ecstasy at the image of Christ they have detected in its features. Lastly, behind them, there is Hogarth himself, innocently sketching the scene, and on the point of being arrested, a hand on his shoulder, a pike above his head.

Two arches frame all these figures, one at the front, which effectively houses the viewer, representing a gloomy opening in the sixteenth-century ramparts that encircled the town, and one at the back representing the old city gate, the Porte du Havre, with a raven perched ominously on top. This arrangement invites many readings. The frontmost opening acts as a proscenium arch, thus placing Hogarth's characters on a stage. Hogarth is here, as in many of his paintings, playing with ideas of reality and illusion, actor and character. At the same time, the two systems of fortification symbolise the tyranny under which all Frenchmen live; it is surely no coincidence that while the bottom half of the gate and everything in front of it are cast in shadow, the top half, bearing the English coat of arms, is bathed in gorgeous evening light. The sun of English freedom has set, leaving France in the dark. The architecture of the painting, however, also invites another still more subtle reading. Hogarth has painted the gate to look like a mouth, its portcullis representing teeth, the drawbridge a tongue. Understood in this way, the 'stage' on which the main action takes place is in fact the inside of a mouth, and the darkened arch at the forefront, a throat. *The Gate of Calais* is clearly about food – everyone in it, apart from Hogarth, is hungry. It is not so often recognised, however, that it is painted, quite literally, from the stomach's point of view.

The Gate of Calais is not one of Hogarth's most likeable paintings, yet whatever one feels about its crowing chauvinism, the painting, with its gates and archways, guns and pikes, walls and bars, open skies and dark corners, retains a haunting, dream-like power. It is not easily forgotten. It certainly made an impression on Hogarth's contemporaries. He quickly turned it into a best-selling print, sold under the title of Fielding's song, *O the Roast Beef of Old England.* One indication of the extent of its popularity is provided by a pamphlet that appeared in 1767, three years after Hogarth's death, which contains a description of the furnished room of an unmarried clerk in a public office, who could only afford to live in a meaner part of town. Despite his poverty, however, the room contained 'two large prints cut in wood and coloured, framed with deal but not glazed, viz. 1. Hogarth's Gate of Calais. 2. Queen Esther and Ahasuerus'.[4] The painting also appeared on the side of bowls and other earthenware vessels – indeed, one patriotic Englishman, working for the East India Company in China, even had it copied on to a large porcelain bowl made in Canton.[5] Theodosius Forrest, the author of the Sublime Society of Beefsteaks' *The Song of the Day*, wrote a long and witty cantata about the painting, performed at the Haymarket Theatre. Here is Forrest's crowing depiction of the French soldier with the bayonet on his back and bowl of gruel in his hand:

RECITATIVE
A half-Starv'd Soldier, shirtless, pale and lean,
Who such a Sight before had never seen,
Like Garrick's frighten'd Hamlet, gaping stood,
And gaze'd with Wonder at the British Food.
His Morning's Mess forsook the friendly Bowl,
And in small Streams along the Pavement stole:

He heav'd a sigh, which gave his Heart Relief,
And then in plaintive Tone declare'd his Grief.

AIR
A sacré Dieu! Vat do I see yonder?
Dat looks so tempting, red and vhite?
Begar I see it is de roast Beef from Londre.
Oh grant me one letel Bite.[6]

Strangely perhaps, *The Gate of Calais* was the first painting by Hogarth to exploit the symbolic significance of food, the hint of an allusion in *Noon* excepted. You might have expected a man who had grown up among the sheep and cows of Smithfield, who had pilloried French painting and Italian opera again and again, and who had been attending the Sublime Society of Beefsteaks on a weekly basis since 1735, to have incorporated food and drink into his satires earlier. Nevertheless, after the Calais painting, he did begin to use these as an easy way of getting across his message about England and her neighbours. Two pairs of paintings from the 1750s, in particular, stand out.

One of these pairs – *The Invasion* – offers little more than a cruder, more didactic treatment of themes Hogarth had already covered in *The March to Finchley* and *The Gate of Calais*. The peace that had allowed Hogarth to visit France in 1748 proved short lived. Hostilities broke out again, principally over Canada, in 1755, marking the beginning of the Seven Years War a year later. Events moved slowly. Then suddenly, in March, news arrived of the massing of French soldiers in Le Havre and Brest, causing another burst of panic across Britain. Hogarth responded quickly, with two prints, 'France' and 'England', whose upbeat mood contrasted with other, more fearful prints of the time.

Advertised by Hogarth as being 'proper to be stuck up in public places', these were bold efforts at popular propaganda. The first shows the French preparing to embark for England. In the background, troops are forced, at pike-point, on to a ship. In the foreground a group of emaciated soldiers look on as a monk loads a cart with instruments of torture, religious icons and a plan for the erection of a monastery at Blackfriars, London. On one side, a modishly dressed officer roasts a few frogs over a fire. Behind them, a crude inn, more like a prison, with the sign of a wooden shoe and a joint of meatless beef ribs hanging on a hook, advertises the inevitable *soupe maigre*. The rousing verses underneath, written by Hogarth's friend Garrick, made the message explicit:

With lanthern jaws, and croaking Gut
See how the half-starved Frenchmen strut,
And call us English Dogs!
But soon we'll teach these bragging Foes,
That Beef & Beer give heavier Blows
Than Soup and Roasted frogs.

The second print, this time of England, depicts a happier scene. Once again, troops mass in the background – this time voluntarily. To the right, a young volunteer, with good sturdy English calves, not unlike Hogarth's own, stands on tiptoes so as to pass a height test. To the left, in front of a rich, solid tavern, offering meat 'roast and boiled everyday', a group of English troops make merry with a couple of buxom country girls. The table in front of them carries further manifestations of English plenty in the form of a tankard brimming with beer and a round of beef. Hogarth has one of the soldiers painting a crude caricature of the French king, with sword and

William Hogarth, *The Invasion*, Plate I 'France', 1756

gallows, on the tavern wall – an ironic allusion, perhaps, to his own role as propagandist. The sun shines, a royal standard flutters in the breeze, and a young, happy fifer plays *God Save the King* on his pipe. After the complexity of *The March to Finchley* or *The Gate of Calais,* these two prints seem a little crude. As propaganda, however, they were effective enough, and, although the threatened invasion never came, were later adapted for use as recruitment posters.

The second pair of prints to take up the subject of food had, like *The Invasion,* a specific social purpose. Published in 1751, *Gin Lane* and *Beer Street* were aimed at combating the terrible scourge of gin drinking that had London, and beyond it the country at large, by the throat. It has been estimated that in the parish of St Giles alone, the square where Hogarth would set his prints, a quarter of the houses sold gin,

William Hogarth, *Gin Lane*, 1751

BEER STREET.
Beer, happy Produce of our Isle
Can sinewy Strength impart,
And wearied with Fatigue and Toil
Can chear each manly Heart.
Labour and Art upheld by Thee
Successfully advance,
We quaff Thy balmy Juice with Glee
And Water leave to France.
Genius of Health, thy grateful Taste
Rivals the Cup of Jove,
And warms each English generous Breast
With Liberty and Love.

William Hogarth, *Beer Street*, 1751

'beside about 82 twopenny houses of the greatest infamy where gin was the liquor drunk'. Gin was the coke, smack and crack of the eighteenth century, only worse. It was entirely in character that Hogarth, whose work, as he got older, became increasingly didactic, should have put his pen to use in this way. His first print depicts the city ravished by liquor: at the centre of this concrete, locatable version of hell, a ragged, drunken mother, her breasts shamelessly exposed to public view, sways on the edge of unconsciousness, as her baby falls to its death from her arms. To the right, another mother pours gin down her child's throat, while desperate for a drink, destitute citizens hand their last possessions to a pawnbroker. In the background, families bury their loved ones among the ruins of the city. Only the walls of the pawnbroker and undertaker's, with their aggressive, thrusting signs, stand firm.

If *Gin Lane* depicts a city on the point of death, *Beer Street* hums with life. Gin has been replaced by beer. Result: health, wealth and happiness. Two jovial tradesmen, a butcher and a blacksmith, each with their aprons and hats, and telltale tools, drink overflowing tankards of foaming English porter. A Union Jack flies smartly from St Martin-in-the-Fields and the pawnbroker's alone is on the verge of collapse. In what is perhaps another joke at his own expense, Hogarth has included one ragged figure: an artist reduced to painting a tavern sign. There is no need, and therefore no market, for edifying moral satire here.

It would be wrong to see *Beer Street* as a paean to beer alone. It is also a brazen advertisement for native produce generally – especially for English food. The problem with the London of the first print is that it has succumbed to a foreign drink – as everyone knew, gin arrived from Holland with Prince William late in the seventeenth century – rather than remaining loyal to English traditions. As a consequence, everyone is hungry: the man at the bottom of the stairs is about to expire from starvation; another fights with a dog for a bone. More or less all the figures in *Beer Street,* by comparison, are fat and contented, and no wonder: their world flows with home-grown goods. The two street sellers in the centre, their baskets piled high with fish, mirror the tradesmen on the left, with brimming tankards. Behind the fishwives, a pretty servant girl, enjoying the attentions of an amorous road builder, carries a basket of vegetables from market. The fat blacksmith holds a large joint of meat aloft in the air, as if it were an English standard – although in this case it looks more like a leg of mutton than a sirloin of beef. Like *The Gate of Calais, Beer Street* is a bold declaration of culinary patriotism.

8

Bulldogs

Well of all the dogs it stands confessed,
Your English Bulldogs are the best.

Christopher Smart, 'The English Bulldog, Dutch Mastiff and Quail', *Fables,* 1765

ENGLISHMEN TOOK PRIDE in being great beef eaters, but they were also known for their bulldogs – dogs used for bull and bear baiting. By 1750, beef and bulldogs, already connected in Shakespeare's *Henry V,* had become inextricably linked symbols of masculine, meaty, English virtue.

Animal baiting in England stretches back at least to Roman times. If it ever stopped, it was firmly established again by the twelfth century, and seems to have grown in popularity through the Plantagenet and Tudor periods, when it became a regular entertainment at court. The royal office of 'bearward', or bear keeper, dates from at least the beginning of Richard III's reign in 1483. His successor, Henry VII, having witnessed a lion bait, is said to have ordered that all baiting dogs in the kingdom, 'how many soever they were in number', should be hanged, so strongly did he object to seeing common curs defeating 'the valiant lyon, King of al beastes'.[1] But both Henry VIII and Queen Elizabeth, the latter famous for her masculine tastes, patronised what became known as the 'royal sport', laid on at Christmas, Whitsun and other holidays, and in honour of visiting ambassadors and royalty. On 25 May 1559, French ambassadors dined with Elizabeth and 'after dener to bear and bull baytyng, and the Quens grace and the embassadurs stod in the galere lokyng of the pastym'.[2] James I continued the tradition. After the ball held at Whitehall to celebrate the end of hostilities between England and Spain in 1604, Juan Fernandez de Velasco, Constable of Castile, reported, 'all then took their places at the windows of the room which looked out upon a square, where a platform was raised, and a vast crowd had assembled to see the King's bears fight with hounds. This afforded great amusement. Presently, a bull, tied to the end of a rope, was fiercely baited by dogs.'[3]

The sport was not the preserve of royalty. Mid-sixteenth-century prints of London show two large 'bayting' rings, one for 'bolles' one for 'beares', at Bankside, on the south side of the Thames, in Tudor times an insalubrious area famous for its taverns, brothels and theatres, as well as its baiting rings. The rings and the animals baited in them were held on a patent by the royal bearward, or 'the Master of the Game', who had the right to lay on regular public baits for his own profit. If the animals were wanted at court, they were shipped by river from their home in Bankside.

The Bankside baitings took place two or three times a week, on Wednesdays, Thursdays and Sundays, and featured prominently in foreign travellers' accounts of London, where they were often seen as an expression of a characteristically English love of physical exertion and cruel games. 'The common people' of England, Muralt wrote in the 1720s, 'have a great many diversions which may serve to let them know themselves'.

> Some have the appearance of fierceness: as that of throwing cocks at some distance. Another great diversion is to [watch] either men or beasts fighting, where there is always bloodshed. There is another very troublesome and insolent; this is football, where they take a great deal of pleasure in breaking windows and coach glasses if they meet any; or when there is any public rejoicing, they make a line, and toss people passing by, to and again.[4]

Arriving in London from Scotland in 1762, James Boswell enthusiastically adapted himself to his surroundings. As his *London Journal* made clear, this entailed eating great quantities of meat, but it also meant participating in the playful torture of innocent animals:

> The enemies of the people of England who would have them considered in the worst light represent them as selfish, beef-eaters and cruel. In this view I resolved today to be a true-born Old Englishman. I went to the City to Dolly's Steak-house in Paternoster Row and swallowed my dinner by myself to fulfil the charge of selfishness; I had a large fat beef-steak to fulfil the charge of beef-eating; and I went at five o'clock to the Royal Cockpit in St James' Park and saw cockfighting for about seven hours to fulfil the charge of cruelty.[5]

The English passion for fox hunting was – and, controversially, still is – another manifestation of this devotion to violent sports.

Puritans had long campaigned against animal baiting – though less, the historian Lord Macaulay famously suggested, 'because it gave pain to the bear', than 'because it gave pleasure to the spectators' – and succeeded in having it banned under the Commonwealth. Charles II, however, lost no time in rehabilitating the sport, and the old bear garden was back in operation within a few years of the Restoration.

During the eighteenth century baiting rings opened in Marylebone Gardens and at Cokley-in-the-Hole, Clerkenwell, and fights were staged on a less formal basis at London markets, festivals and frost fairs.

The capital was not the only place where one could see animals baited in Tudor, Stuart or Georgian England. Almost every large town in the country played host to bear or, more regularly, bull baits (the cheaper, repertory version of the sport). It provided a common diversion at many church wakes, fairs and public holidays or harvest festivities, but was also all but required by statute: it was widely believed that baiting bulls softened their flesh, and many English towns had laws forbidding butchers from selling meat from uncastrated bulls unless the bull had been baited to death.

Having completed the marling of his fields in 1712, Nicholas Blundell 'Baited a Large Bull in the Bottom of my new Marl-pit in the Great Morehey, he was never baited before as I know off, yet played to admiration . . .'.[6] When the road connecting Marlborough to Bristol was finished in 1736, Squire John Smith, a local landlord, laid on two days of bull baiting, as well as 'Backsword, Wrestling, Bowling and Dancing' by way of celebration. On the third day 'the Bull was divided by Mr Smith amongst his poor Neighbours on the Top of the Hill, where they diverted themselves with Bonfires, Ale and Roast beef for several hours and concluded with drinking the Royal Family's and several other loyal Healths'.[7]

By mid-century progressive London opinion had turned against animal baiting – Hogarth condemned it, along with other species of violence, in *The Four Stages of Cruelty*, a print series of 1751 showing how enjoyment in the suffering of animals led on to still worse vices. But baiting remained a feature of the country scene, popular with squires, yeomen and labourers alike. In 1759 James Woodforde reported going

Bull baiting, *c.*1820. Note these dogs' long muzzles, relatively long legs and lithe bodies. The modern 'English bulldog', with its shortened muzzle, bow-legs and barrel chest was a confection of nineteenth-century fanciers, who bred their dogs for show, not for fighting.

to a 'Bear-baiting in Ansford', his father's parish, and doesn't seem to have disapproved of the spectacle.[8]

As the survival of Birmingham's 'Bull Ring' and 'Bull Street' testify, bull baiting was particularly popular in the Midlands. Tutbury in Staffordshire and Stamford in Lincolnshire both held annual bull runs – basically free-for-all, weaponless bullfights that attracted hundreds of spectators from neighbouring areas. Shakespeare, a Midlander himself, managed to work in an allusion to the national passion for animal baiting in the exchanges from *Henry V*, with which this book began. The French lord, Orléans, having heard mention of England's valiant mastiffs, dismisses their owners as 'Foolish curs, that run winking into the mouth of a Russian bear and have their heads crushed like rotten apples'.[9] It was a sly allusion to a sport that his audience would have identified, like beef, apples and courage, as characteristically English.

The most detailed description of a bull bait was provided by the ever-observant Henri Misson at the very end of the seventeenth century. The bull having been tied to a rope of about fifteen feet, fastened to a ring in the ground, the first dog was let loose:

> The dog runs at the Bull; the Bull, immovable, looks down upon the Dog with an Eye of Scorn, and only turns a Horn to him to hinder him from coming near: the Dog is not daunted by this, he runs round him, and tries to get beneath his Belly, in order to seize him by the Muzzle or the Dewlap [throat] or the pendant Glands [testicles]. . . . The Bull then puts himself into a posture of Defence; he beats the Ground with his feet, which he joins together as close as possible, and his chief aim is not to gore the dog with the Point of his Horn, but to slide one of them under the Dog's Belly (who creeps close to the ground to hinder it) and to throw him so high in the Air that he may break his neck in the Fall. This

> often happens: . . . but sometimes too, he fastens upon his Enemy, and when once he has seiz'd him with his Eye-teeth, he sticks to him like a Leech, and would sooner die than leave his hold. . . . In the End, either the Dog tears out the Piece he has laid Hold on, and falls, or else remains fix'd to him, with an Obstinacy that would never end, if they did not pull him off.[10]

There were, naturally, variations on this spectacle. Sometimes several beasts were baited together and bets placed on which would die last. Sometimes fireworks were strapped to the back of a bull or a cat tied to its tail.*

Bear and bull baiting required a bear or a bull but it also required a dog. More precisely, a bulldog – a short-legged, broad-chested, wide-mouthed, tough-skinned and furiously tenacious canine, with the courage and agility to get underneath a bull, grab it by the neck or the stomach and cling on, come what may. Baiting's large-scale revival in the medieval period encouraged the breeding of fighting dogs and led to an identification of them as peculiarly English. So when in the 1570s Johannes Caius agreed to the request of a Scottish friend, and wrote an account *Of Englishe Dogges,* he included a section on the mastiff, which explained how its natural 'violence and valliance' was cultivated by 'Our English men', who

* One especially enterprising early eighteenth-century London fair manager placed a notice promising: '. . . a mad bull to be dressed up with fireworks and turned loose in the game place, a dog to be dressed up with fireworks over him, a bear to be let loose at the same time, and a cat to be tied to the bull's tail, a mad bull to be dressed up with fireworks to be baited' (1729, quoted in W.E.H. Lecky, *A History of England in the Eighteenth Century,* 1920, vol. II, pp. 195–6).

> teach theyr dogges to baite the Bear, to baite the Bull and other such cruel and bloody beastes . . . and oftentimes they traine them up in fighting and wrestling with a man having for safeguard of his lyfe, either a Pickestaffe, a clubbe or a sworde, and by using them to such exercises as these, theyr dogges become sturdy and strong. The force which is in them surmounteth all belief. The fast holde which they take with their teeth exceedeth all credit, three of them against a beare, fowre [four] against a lion are sufficient.[11]

According to the patriotic William Harrison, who endorsed Caius' account of the 'courage of our mastiffs', the Elizabethan politician Thomas Sackville was so proud of England's fighting dogs that, sent on a diplomatic mission to the French court in 1571, he took a champion dog with him and laid on a demonstration before the French king: 'alone and without any help at all', it 'pulled down first an huge bear, then a pard [leopard], and last of all a lion'.[12] English pluck beats French might! It was the Battle of Agincourt all over again.

Bankside, England's leading baiting ring, was naturally renowned for its bulldogs. From 1598 the office of bearward was joined to that of 'Keeper of the Bandogs and Mastiffs', with a fee of 10d a day for exercising this office. Lupold von Wedel, who attended the games at Bankside in August 1584, reported that kennels next to the ring contained 'about a hundred large English dogs, with separate wooden kennels for each of them'.[13] But animals were reared and trained all over the country, particularly in the Midlands – hence the 'Staffordshire bull-terrier', said to date from the late eighteenth century, when the bulldog was crossed with the now extinct white terrier in order to produce a fighting dog with a long and more punishing head. Bankside seems to have been something of an exception in keeping its own dogs. Generally, those organising a fight supplied the beasts to be baited –

often butchers, who sold the meat – while the public at large brought along the dogs.

So it was that by the beginning of the seventeenth century the ferocity of the English bulldogs was another national peculiarity – along with a fondness for meat and an appetite for physical exercise – that foreigners commented on. Visiting London in 1598, the German Paul Hentzner, whom we have already met praising the English way with roast meat, significantly described the bulldog as 'the *English* bulldog', confirming that it was already a thing for which the English were widely known. A hundred and fifty years later, the Scottish philosopher David Hume observed that 'the courage of bulldogs and game cocks seems peculiar to England'.[14] Indeed, by the eighteenth century, foreigners were drawing comparisons between the English bulldog and its owners. 'Their dogs are, I believe', the Swiss traveller Muralt remarked in the 1720s, 'the boldest in the world, and . . . the least bragging':

> They neither bark nor bite and fight to the death without any noise. One may see some of these creatures dragging along a broken leg and returning to the charge. I am assur'd that one of them, in King Charles II's time, killed a lion, and that it has been proved by Experience, that such as are a true breed will suffer their legs to be cut off, one after another, without letting off their hold. If I durst, I would readily say, that there's a strong resemblance in many things between the English and their dogs. Both are silent, headstrong, lazy, unfit for fatigue, no way quarrelsome, intrepid, eager in fight, insensible of blows and incapable of parting.[15]

It is hardly surprising then that the bulldog became, in the early eighteenth century, a familiar icon in anti-court, anti-French propaganda. It was employed in 1729, for instance, by *The Craftsman*, the most influential opposition journal of its day, and one that did more than any other to spread the view that Walpole and his government were ruthlessly set on undermining centuries of English prosperity and freedom. One letter – clearly the work of the editor – found a playful way of fitting the bulldog into this nostalgic scheme. The correspondent began with an elaborate appreciation of 'that ancient, genuine Race of true-bred English Bull-Dogs, who were not only famous at home, but likewise acquired a glorious Reputation abroad, excelling in fight, victorious over their enemies, undaunted in death; and in the midst of crackling Blazes and artificial Thunders, resolutely continuing tenacious to the last'. But he also lamented the fact that more recently certain cruel and lazy masters had attempted to harness the bulldog to a carriage; the fact that they had succeeded was a sad

Bull Baiting, **Henry Thomas Alken, *c.*1820, Stapleton Collection**

Anon., ***The Gallic Cock and English Lyon,*** **1739**

indication that the 'Race now surviving' was a 'mungrel Race' – the bulldog of old would never have submitted 'to this vile servitude'.[16]

The bulldog was used to similar purpose in mid-eighteenth-century satirical prints. He crops up, for instance, in *The Gallic Cock and English Lyon,* a satire on Walpole's failure to stand up to France and Spain in the War of Jenkins' Ear of 1739, which shows a bulldog, symbol of English courage, chained to a stake and so unable to protect the English lion from being blinded by a French cock.

The symbol is employed again in *Court and Country United against the Popish Invasion,* a celebration of the British people's calm courage when faced with the prospect of a French invasion in early 1744: the king and his two sons, the Prince of Wales and the Duke of Cumberland, sit in state, flanked on one side by peers kneeling, swords drawn, vowing to support the king 'with our lives', and on the other by citizens and

David Jones, *The Whipping Post*, 1762

clergy, pledging loyalty and 'our fortunes'; two pictures hang on a wall behind them, one showing 'English bulldogs' tearing a cur to pieces, the other the same dogs standing up to 'the Pope's bull', a punning reference to a papal bull supporting the young Pretender's claim to the British throne.

The symbol is still being used two decades later, in *The Whipping Post*, an etching aimed at Lord Bute, George III's much hated favourite, which depicts a kilted Scotsman – Bute – flogging the naked Britannia with a large thistle, while a tethered bulldog, desperate to save her, barks and bounds helplessly nearby:

> *The Bull-dog, as well as to bark, may go whistle,*
> Britannia *was doom'd to be flogg'd with a Thistle.*

By this time, moreover, the association between bulldogs, bulls and beef, made earlier by Shakespeare, had taken firm root. Both the London butcher, who emerges in prints of this time as an early cartoon Englishman (of whom more in the next chapter) and John Bull, who evolved a little later, were typically depicted with a bulldog at their side and a joint of beef nearby. Beef, bulls and bulldogs, after all, not only stood for the same supposedly characteristically Protestant English traits of directness, determination and courage (English satirists, by contrast, generally used cocks, monkeys or foxes to depict the hungry, vain, scheming and lascivious Frenchman). They were related through the fact that bulls and bulldogs looked alike, and were pitted together in the baiting ring – and that the fight tended to result in copious quantities of honest tender English meat.

9

Butchers

In France the people sing to amuse themselves, and here they pass their time in boxing.

L'Abbé Le Blanc, *Letters on the English and French Nations,* Vol. I, 1747

AT SOME POINT in the late 1740s or early 1750s – the exact date is not known – an artist and engraver called Anthony Walker issued a lively, complex little print, *The Beaux Disaster.* Set in Butcher's Row, a street lined with butcher shops that ran from one of the City's principal gates, Temple Bar, to the Strand, London's most fashionable shopping spot, it depicted the aftermath of an encounter between a Frenchified fop and an English butcher. The fop, identified in the print's caption as 'poor Fribble', a mincing little thing with huge cuffs and shiny white stockings, had wandered among England's working people, and, having offended the butcher, is shown hanging humiliated from a hook, alongside joints of meat. The triumphant butcher and his dog, standing at the very centre of the picture, taunt him, while a varied crowd of shopkeepers, prostitutes, and well-dressed sightseers enjoy the spectacle.

The Beaux Disaster works as an ingenious social satire. The beau, we can take it, is a great consumer of clothes, luxurious food and women;

The BEAUX DISASTER.
Ye Smarts whose Merit lies in Dress,
Take warning by a Beaux Distress,
Whose Pigmy Size & ill-tim'd Rage
Ventur'd with Butchers to engage.
But they unus'd Affronts to brook,
Have hung poor Fribble on a Hook,
While, foul Disgrace, expos'd in Air,
The Butchers shout, & Ladies stare.
Satyr so strong, ye Fops, must strike you
How can you think ye Fair will like you,
Women of Sense, in Men despise
The Anticks, they in Monkeys prize.

Anthony Walker, *The Beaux Disaster*, c.1747

his elaborately worked appearance is intended to signify his wealth and sophistication. Here, though, his world is turned upside down and he finds himself reduced to the level (and Walker manages to make all these equations at one and the same time) of mannequin, tavern sign, puppet, sex object and piece of meat. The fashion setter has become a fashion victim.[1]

The print also invites a more political reading. Temple Bar had a special space in London's politics. The gate itself, marking the passage from the toiling City to the aristocratic West End, was crowned with spikes, on which the heads of rebels and traitors were customarily impaled. The space in front of it had long been the focus of popular celebrations and demonstrations – a place where political bills, newssheets and prints were posted, and effigies of the Pope, Guy Fawkes or the Pretender paraded and burned. Walker's print did not include any effigies (other, that is, than poor Fribble turned mannequin) but he did include the rotting heads of two of the rebels who had been executed for supporting the Catholic uprisings of '45 – one can just make them out to the left of the frontmost tavern sign. The scene at the centre of the print, then, can been read as an allusion to the scene at the back: the victory of patriotic Englishmen over the Stuart Pretender is figured in the victory of the manly butcher over the effeminate fop.

Walker was evidently a talented artist and it is pity that so little is known about him. But it is enough here to note that his print, in depicting a confrontation between a butcher and a fop, represents an early contribution to the emergence of the English butcher as a stock character of late eighteenth-century satirical art. This, in turn, helped the butcher on his way to becoming, for a short time at least, a leading emblem of Englishness – a forerunner of John Bull – and an important component of England's roast beef cult.

The Beaux Disaster evinces a widely shared pride in the freedom and informality of English manners, and the democratic character of English street life. Where the French, or so the English liked to tell themselves, were expected to grovel to their superiors, the English met each other as equals as freeborn Englishmen.

There was some justification for this pride. As foreign travellers noted, exchanges between the rich and the poor were remarkably uninhibited by considerations of rank. Misson reported with some surprise that 'there are cook shops in all parts of the town, where it was very common to go and choose upon the spit the part [of meat] you like and eat it there. A Frenchman of any distinction would think it a great scandal in France to be seen to eat in such a place . . . but in England they laugh at such niceties.'[2] The Swiss traveller Muralt later made the same point when, having described the 'common people's'

Henry Bunbury, *View on the Pont Neuf*, 1771

taste for sports and violent exercise, he went on to suggest that 'Many of these diversions are proof of their happy condition, since even some grandees partake in them. You may see blue garters [noblemen] pass the time at bowls with tradesmen, without any distinction, which shows not only that greatness among the English is no hindrance to amusements but likewise that it does not consist in contempt for the populace.'[3] Writing in the 1780s, the German visitor J.W. von Archenholz confirmed that the English 'people in general testify but little respect for their superiors' – indeed that the 'very majesty of the throne is not always sufficiently respected'.

> No minister . . . no grandee of the kingdom will pretend to make any of the populace give way to him in the street; and notwithstanding this, they every day walk through the most crowded part of the metropolis, where

> they find themselves splashed, squeezed and elbowed, without having the least wish to complain.[4]

Nowhere, as contemporaries affirmed, was this relative freedom of manners more evident than in the frequency with which noblemen and commoners came to blows. As Misson further observed, a nobleman and a coachman who disagreed about a fare would not hesitate to fight it out, bulldog to bulldog.[5]

Not only visitors from abroad, but native Britons too were sometimes provoked or embarrassed by these excesses – it was often said that, if the French populace was too subservient, the English was not subservient enough. Nevertheless, patriotically minded Englishmen tended to comfort themselves with the argument that the unruliness of the English – the jeering, the punching, the cat throwing and animal baiting – was not so much, as the critics claimed, an indictment of English liberty as its condition. 'They who complain in peace of the insolence of the populace, must remember', as Dr Johnson admonished, 'that their insolence is bravery in war.'[6] 'Crowd' was just the collective noun for 'free born Englishmen'.

Perhaps it is not surprising that, at least from the 1740s onwards, patriotic writings and art abound in depictions, at once both comic and proud, of English crowds and English street scenes, and, more particularly, in imagined encounters between snooty fops and lowly Englishmen – encounters in which, as in Walker's print, the Englishman always triumphs.[7] Walker's work, in fact, appears to have been partly inspired by a story centred on just this sort of encounter that had appeared a few years earlier, in 1747, in *The British Magazine*. 'A Beau's Sunday Morning Walk' recounted the 'very extraordinary series of adventures' endured by one Charles Bagatelle, an aristocratic dandy, while walking from the West End to a rendezvous in Covent Garden.

At first the initiative lies with Bagatelle, who, dressed in the height of fashion, loudly scoffs at the outmoded attire of a group of Quaker churchgoers. Soon, however, the tables are turned, as Bagatelle finds himself stuck in a crowded alley of greasy cookshops, where he suffers the indignity of being confronted with 'a smoaking buttock of Beef' and a 'dap of pudding', while the dirty multitude looks on and laughs. The final humiliation comes when a common whore, standing in for the usual butcher, leans out of a window and empties a dirty bowl of water on to his beautifully curled ringlets.*[8] *Sal Dab giving Monsieur a Receipt in Full,* a 1776 print depicting an English fishwife beating up an overdressed Frenchman, offers another version of the same scenario. The Frenchman, having taken off his coat, reveals the superficiality of his appearance; his shirt consists only of cuffs and collar, and his breeches have no seat, thus exposing his *derrière.*

Walker's *Beaux Disaster,* then, belongs to a tradition of art that celebrated the relatively informal, democratic nature of English common life and the well-fed insolence of ordinary English people. Walker, however, did not pick *any* figure as the representative Englishman; he picked the butcher. Here, too, he was working within a well-defined convention, for English butchers were frequently taken as embodiments of brave, manly Englishness.

Again, there was some warrant for this in the realities of eighteenth-century English life: if a fop was going to be attacked, likely as not he was going to be attacked by a member of the meat trade. Most eighteenth-century London artisans and craftsmen

*Sam Foote's chauvinist satire, *The Englishman Return'd from Paris,* of 1756, includes a similar encounter. The play opens with the Frenchified Buck having returned from Paris to London, intent on seducing the virtuous English fiancée who has been faithfully awaiting his return. The effect of his grand entrance, however, is somewhat spoilt by his appearing covered in coal – a coal merchant had got the better of him on the street.

Anon., *Sal Dab giving Monsieur a Receipt in Full*, 1766

belonged to one trade guild or another, qualifying them as 'freemen', or citizens of the City of London. Part-college, part-trade union, part-social club, each guild had its own system of apprenticeship, its own meeting hall, and its peculiar ceremonial and festive traditions, all of which worked to bind fellow tradesmen together. Although not one of the leading guilds in terms of wealth or prestige, the Butchers' Company nevertheless possessed a particularly strong sense of identity; its members had a long-established reputation for loud, manly irreverence. The Butchers of Clare Market, between Covent Garden and Temple Bar, and those of the neighbouring Butcher's Row, were known as the loudest and most irreverent of all – 'the arbiters of the galleries, the leaders of theatrical rows, the musicians at actresses' marriages, the chief mourners at players' funerals'.[9] Bull and bear baits, cock fights and other cruel sports, often identified at home and abroad as characteristically English, were generally run by butchers – and it was their dogs that tended to dominate the ring.*

Butchers also had a reputation as mean prizefighters – 1750 saw a famous victory of Slack 'the Butcher', over the long-reigning champion Broughton, a waterman. (The king's son, the Duke of Cumberland, was in the audience, although his French equivalent would never have been seen at such a plebeian spectacle.)[10] When an unpopular public figure feared attack from the crowd, as Lord Bute, George III's Scottish Prime Minister did in 1761, he hired 'a guard of butchers and bruisers' to protect him.[11] Butchers generally took a leading role in popular festivities and patriotic celebrations, usually announcing their presence by banging together cleavers and marrowbones, a practice that can be

*The Company of Butchers was, in the Tudor period, expressly charged with donating offal and waste to feed the wretched beasts at Bankside; when baiting was revived in 1660, the Company was instructed to return to this old practice. The meat was rowed across the Thames from the markets of Eastcheap and Newgate in two boats every night.

traced back to the skimmingtons, or 'rough music', of earlier centuries, when cuckolds and female adulterers were made the object of public mockery. Writing in 1827, but looking back to a time before the French Revolution, the radical writer and publisher William Hone recalled how on Guy Fawkes Day,

> the butchers in Clare-market had a bonfire in the open space of the market, next to the Bear[-baiting] Yard and they thrashed each other 'round about the wood-fire' with the . . . sinews of slaughtered bulls. Large parties of butchers from all the markets paraded the streets, ringing peals from marrow bones and cleavers, so loud as to overpower the storms of sound that came from the rocking belfries of the churches. By ten o'clock, London was so lit up by bonfires and fireworks, that from the suburbs it looked in one red heat.[12]

And butchers were inevitably associated with that icon of Englishness, roast beef. No wonder they were often seen, and saw themselves, as having a privileged relationship with the nation.

If Hogarth's paintings and prints offer a rich source of patriotic images of English food, they also abound in more or less approving images of the free, unruly English crowd in general and of London butchers in particular. *Industry and Idleness,* a series of prints produced at around the time of *The March to Finchley* and *The Gate of Calais,* charting the contrasting fates of two fellow apprentices, Goodchild and Idle – Goodchild rises to become Lord Mayor, Idle ends his life on the gallows – provides several examples. The sixth print depicts Goodchild on his wedding day. Having completed his apprenticeship, he has married his master's daughter and been offered a partnership in his profitable weaving business. Not even the most privileged Londoners, however, could ever hope to escape the din of the London crowd: as the newlyweds sip their expensive tea, Goodchild pays the musicians who have gathered outside the window to celebrate the marriage. And the band includes not only drummers and cellists, but a gang of butchers with marrowbones and cleavers – young apprentice butchers were known for their skill with these instruments, and working in groups of four or eight, with each boy's cleaver sharpened to give out a different note, often supplied a musical accompaniment to wedding parties.

The last print in the series, *The Industrious 'Prentice Lord Mayor of London,* provides a similar image: the Lord Mayor's Procession, an important day in London's festive calendar, in which Goodchild, the new mayor, rides triumphant in the mayor's gilded coach. The city's

William Hogarth, *Industry & Idleness,* Plate 5, 'The Industrious 'Prentice out of his Time, and Married to his Master's Daughter'.

constables and guilds leaders, magistrates and aldermen, sheriffs and the officers march before him. But Hogarth's print gives pride of place not to these representatives of hierarchy and order, but to the cheering, jostling crowd surrounding the coach – a crowd that appears here, as it does in *The March to Finchley,* as an ambiguous force, at once joyful and menacing, free and licentious. And butchers, with their telltale aprons and sharpening irons, are notably prominent within it, pushing from the outside towards the centre of the scrum.

After his appearance in both Hogarth's and Walker's prints the virile, assertive butcher became something of a staple of eighteenth-century graphic satire, being called on again and again in the fight against aristocratic haughtiness and foreign arrogance. A flurry of prints circa 1770, for instance, re-imagine the encounter between butcher and fop – or butcher and 'macaroni' as the fop had come to be called, on account of his taste for foreign food. In *English Funn or Docking the Macaroni,* a butcher, his meat hanging proudly behind him, uses his dirty knife to cut away at a Macaroni's hairpiece. Two female street sellers sit beneath a sign for 'fine pud[ding]', and enjoy the scene.

In *The Frenchman in London,* by John Collet, a popular graphic satirist in the Hogarthian style, a small but sturdy English butcher challenges an ornamental Frenchman to a fight; although twice the size of the butcher, the Frenchman turns away helplessly. Once again two women, either pedlars or prostitutes, look on, one pulling the Frenchman's pigtail. In the background, a sign above a door reads 'Foreign gentlemen taught English'.

Collet's print seems, in turn, to have inspired another, by one Adam Smith, which first appeared in *The Oxford Magazine,* accompanied by a 'letter' from the artist:

> Sir, Passing one day through a street near Clare-market, I saw a very

John Collet, *The Frenchman in London*, 1770

> curious rencountre between an English Butcher and a French Valet de Chambre. The Butcher happened to rub against Monsieur which greatly enraged him – 'vat you mean, b---e, said he, to rubba your greasy coat against my person?' The Butcher, like a true bulldog, without any kind of preface, put himself in a posture of attack, gave the Frenchman two or three blows, and obliged him to ask pardon for the insult. The terror expressed by the countenance and attitude of Monsieur is easier to be printed than expressed, I have therefore sent a drawing of it to be inserted in your excellent magazine . . .[13]

The drawing itself, much cruder than Collet's, shows a stout butcher, 'like a true bulldog', punching a skinny valet. At the same time, the butcher's dog pisses on the Frenchman's leg and a boy chimneysweep, on the shoulders of a friend, drops a mouse into his

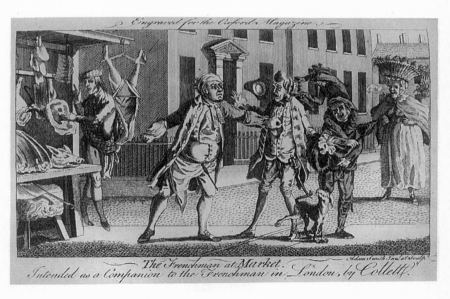

Adam Smith, *The Frenchman at Market*, 1770

wig bag. To the right, the inevitable female street seller looks on amused, while, to the left, a hungry Scotsman steals a piece of meat from the butcher's stall – a typical expression of the virulent anti-Scottish prejudice of the first decade of George III's rule.

None of these prints has anything of Hogarth's anger or humanity: Collet's in particular is typical of the polite, somewhat flaccid social satire that flourished in the trough between Hogarth's death in 1764 and the beginning of the golden age of English graphic satire – the age of Gillray and Rowlandson – in the late 1780s. Yet even these feeble specimens, while inviting us to laugh at the butcher as well the fop, clearly still take a certain pride in the manly irreverence of England's common people.

Such prints show the butcher as archetypal Englishman, standing up to fops, humiliating Frenchmen – and all with roast beef and bulldog at his side – but another class of butcher prints captures the butcher in a different though no less patriotic pose, exercising (and often abusing) his rights as a freeborn Englishman to hold his government to account. They show a radical side to this early embodiment of roast beef-eating Englishness.

Eighteenth-century government was a highly oligarchic affair. Out of a population of roughly ten million, perhaps only three hundred thousand had the franchise, and many of those had little or no choice when it came to casting their vote. And yet, as many foreign observers affirmed, the British political system tolerated, at least by comparison with its continental neighbours, a significant degree of popular participation and protest. Englishmen, and even English women, could follow the news in an extensive and varied press. They could debate affairs of the nation in taverns, coffee shops and clubs, and enjoy the remarkably disrespectful cartoons, squibs, songs and bills put out by rival factions. At election time they were invited to daily speeches, parades, street parties and dinners given by the opposing candidates. And a few constituencies, including Westminster and Middlesex, both close to the centre of power in London, had very extensive franchises – in effect most adult householders, including common tradesmen, could vote. In fact, from the end of the Seven Years War in 1763, through the American War of Independence, to the French Revolution in 1789 – a period of countrywide radical agitation – these constituencies played host to a series of bitterly fought election contests pitting prominent radical 'patriots', most famously the journalist John Wilkes and the aristocrat Charles James Fox, against court candidates.

Wilkes' career proved particularly controversial. A virulent hater of Scotland and most things foreign, he was first prosecuted by the government for criticising the king in 1763. Fleeing to France, he returned to fight the election of 1768, when he was elected to Middlesex, largely on the vote of independent tradesmen and artisans – the 'forty-shilling freeholders'. The government, however, had him expelled from Parliament and imprisoned, moves which provoked riots throughout London and a large national petition. In the course of the next year, Wilkes was elected and expelled three more times, each time to the accompaniment of angry demonstrations and riots.*

* Wilkesite radicalism included a strong strain of culinary chauvinism. Wilkes himself was elected to the Sublime Society of Beefsteaks. His supporters formed at least one similar club, 'The Liberty Beefsteak Club', in his honour. It met in Appleby's Tavern in Parliament Street, which, on Wilkes' release from prison, staged a banquet for its hero, at which roast beef was almost certainly served (see *Cambridge Chronicle*, 14 April 1770). In fact Wilkes' release was greeted with public banquets up and down the country; many would have featured an ox roast (see John Brewer, *Party Ideology and Popular Politics at the Accession of George III*, Cambridge, 1976, pp. 178–9). One pro-Wilkes print maker produced a coat of arms for his hero; it did not feature roast beef, but it did include an 'English Mastiff', which the key describes as 'expressive of fealty, constancy and watchfulness' (BMC 4205).

Despite the oligarchic character of eighteenth-century government, then, there remained a certain scope for popular political involvement. And just as butchers took a lead in London's popular entertainments and festive life, so they played a prominent part in popular politics. It had been butchers, for instance, who had led the popular demonstrations against the revolutionary Rump Parliament in 1660 by roasting rumps of beef and other meat on bonfires to cries of 'No More Rump'. Hogarth himself imagined the scene more than half a century later: in a display of bold, popular self-assertion, the London mob, led by butchers, having hung some effigies of the Rump's leaders from the sides of buildings, carries others to be burnt on a fire.

Seventy years later, it was butchers who led the demonstrations

William Hogarth, 'Burning the Rumps at Temple Bar', ***Hudibras*****, 1726**

against Walpole's 1733 Excise Bill, besieging Parliament to cries of 'No slavery, No Excise, No Wooden Shoes!' ('The Butchers', as one contemporary reported, 'have begun the way to all the rest, for within this today they did all rise upon the excise man.')[14] Butchers played a prominent role in the Wilksite demonstrations of the 1760s. In fact no London political procession or riot was complete without the city's butchers, their cleavers and marrowbones.

It is not unexpected, then, that many, perhaps most, eighteenth-century prints depicting election meetings, political demonstrations and civic processions, show butchers with their characteristic costumes and instruments very much to the fore. To take just one early example, *The British Patriot's Procession* represents the triumphal demonstration that took place when an outspoken government critic and popular hero, Alexander Murray, was released from gaol in 1751 – he had been imprisoned for his part in a tumultuous, divisive Westminster election campaign that in some respects foreshadowed those fought later by Wilkes and Fox. The print shows three coaches passing up St James's Street, and at their front a small band of men sporting striped aprons, marrowbones and cleavers. These are butchers.

One pair of prints, above all, stands out for the way they give pride of place to the butcher, with the emphasis very much on pride. In 1768, nine months after Wilkes was first elected as an MP of Middlesex, and at the height of the popular fury over government attempts to unseat him, a second Middlesex MP died, forcing a bitter by-election contested by a little-known courtier, William Proctor, and a high-profile Wilksite candidate, Sergeant Glynn. Accompanying its coverage of the election, *The Oxford Magazine* printed two crude but vital prints, apparently by the same anonymous hand. The first depicted a riot that occurred in the course of the campaign, after the government party allegedly hired heavies to intimidate voters – at least

Anon., ***The British Patriot's Procession*****, 1751**

one man was killed. It shows a mob with large sticks attacking three common women: a mother with babe in arms, a widow, and a street seller – an established symbol of plebeian liberty. The second, equally partisan, shows a raucous election dinner. On the left, a fat, well-dressed man accepts a bribe from a government agent. On the table in front of him lies a small bird, perhaps the much-mocked ortolan (a small game bird), allegedly beloved of fops. Opposite him, sits a butcher, identifiable by his apron, hat and steel. The centre of the table is taken up with a large, crudely drawn joint of beef, the butcher's preferred dish, while below it the butcher's bulldog gnaws the fat ortolan-eater's foot. In contrast to the fat man, however, the butcher nonchalantly *disdains* a bribe. The prints by Walker, Collet and Smith examined earlier offered a somewhat condescending view of the butcher as a crude and comic, if reliable, friend of liberty. Here, however, he appears as a proud citizen.

An Election Entertainment at Brentford can be said to represent the high point of the butcher's career as a patriotic icon. But it was not his swan song. On the contrary, his popularity with the cartoonists reached its peak some fifteen years later, during the famous Westminster election of 1784. This battle, the most important of the 1784 general election, pitted Charles James Fox against another court-government candidate, Sir Cecil Wray. Fox had recently been forced from government, outmanoeuvred by George III and Pitt the Younger, who together, he now argued, were set on transforming Britain into a despotism. George III and Pitt, in turn, detested Fox. Feelings were running high. Fox was a well-known figure; the most brilliant political performer of his time, he had begun his career as a minister with decidedly 'court' views and

Anon., *The Brentford Election*, 1768

then transformed himself into a radical patriot and, despite his notorious profligacy, a 'man of the people'. His campaign's profile, however, was boosted by the support of the beautiful Georgiana, Duchess of Devonshire, the queen of fashionable society. Day after day the Duchess and her lady friends set out to canvass votes in the squalid lanes and reeking alleys of Covent Garden. Wearing foxtails and with feathers in Fox's colours in their hair, they gave specially struck medals, as well, it was claimed, as bribes and kisses to common, dirty freeholders.

This sort of conduct on the part of one of the highest women in the land was unprecedented and provoked uproar. A deluge of articles, squibs and bills, as well as close to a hundred satirical prints, some attacking, some defending her, flowed from the presses. Many of the

Anon., ***An Election Entertainment at Brentford,*** **1769**

Collings, *Female Influence: or The Devonshire Canvas*, 1784

prints depicted Georgiana in the embrace, often only too literally, of Westminster's butchers.

These prints, the best of them by Thomas Rowlandson, a young cartoonist just beginning to make his name, are intriguingly enigmatic. Almost all those featuring butchers were sponsored by the anti-Fox camp and show Georgiana offering them bribes, kisses, or other sexual favours. Some verge on the pornographic. Georgiana was deeply upset by them, just as many right-thinking moralists were deeply shocked that a woman of Georgiana's standing should monger for votes among the plebs. Yet they are not completely hostile. The government ministers who commissioned them doubtless saw something outrageous in the embrace of a duchess and a butcher, but the artists

Lyford, ***A Certain Dutchess kissing Old Swelter-in-Grease,*** **1784**

who drew them treated the whole affair as a source of mirth. True, the Duchess, with her fine features and expensive clothes, and the butchers, with their crude faces and demotic dress, make unlikely pairings. But neither party is depicted altogether unsympathetically.

The Duchess appears appetisingly buxom, and the butchers tend to stand manly, stout and strong. English artists, after all, had long specialised in approving depictions of the easy manners of the English street and of the proud standing of beefy English butchers. They were not going to stop now.

10

John Bull

The world is a bundle of hay,
Mankind are the asses that pull,
Each tugs in a different way, –
And the greatest of these is John Bull!
Byron, 1821

IN 1835 THE DISTINGUISHED German art historian G.F. Waagen, arrived in England for the first time. Like so many of his educated compatriots, Waagen, the author of *Works of Arts and Artists in England* (1838), was a passionate Anglophile, who admired, even from a distance, the British people's enterprise and wealth, their richly stocked shops and comfortable clubs, their free manners and capacity for self-government. Naturally enough, Waagen embarked on a tour of the nation's major art collections, but he had another goal almost as important. He wanted to see a real, flesh and blood John Bull. After exploring the chophouses of London, the taverns of Oxford and the spas of Bath, he was delighted at last to find the creature he was looking for in a Bristol coffee house:

> From the great respect with which he was received, I concluded that he must be an old and welcome customer. After he had seated himself with

> some difficulty at one of the little tables, he speedily began to attack the cold breakfast before him. I had never before witnessed such a desperate onslaught. His first attack was directed against a piece of roast beef, as being the main body of the enemy, and the principal *pièce de résistance.* He repeated his charges with such vivacity, and at such short intervals, that the large mass was rapidly decreased, to my astonishment, and was soon entirely overcome. . . . It was remarkable, how, while he was devouring one morsel, always accompanied with a large piece of bread, his eyes flashed with fire, looking for the next victim. The quantity of ale with which he washed all down was in due proportion. Profound silence reigned during the whole repast, at which a waiter, ready to attend to every call, looked on at due distance, with almost tragical gravity and profound respect. . . . I thanked my stars for having shown me this specimen.[1]

Waagen was not the only foreigner to conceive the English on the model of John Bull. If, by the nineteenth century, the bulldog and roast beef were already long-established icons of English patriotism, John Bull was a relatively late arrival. His popularity, however, more than made up for his tardiness. During the Revolutionary and Napoleonic Wars (1793–1815), a period when Britain often faced serious threat of invasion from its old French enemy, John Bull emerged as a fresh and powerful archetype – one which shaped the way that the English character was viewed at home and abroad.

John Bull made his first appearance in 1712 in *The History of John Bull,* the work of the Scottish physician and satirist John Arbuthnot (1667–1735). Arbuthnot, like his friend Swift, was a radical, 'country' Tory and his story, charting the ruin of John Bull, a small cloth merchant, in a protracted lawsuit with Nick Frog (the Dutch) and Louis Baboon (the French), worked as an attack on Queen Anne's Whig government – Arbuthnot believed that the Whigs were needlessly prolonging the War of Spanish Succession against France, to the benefit of rich Whig financiers. Animals had long been used to represent national characters and Arbuthnot made use of all the old stereotypes. So Nick Frog is depicted as mean and wily and Louis Baboon inconstant and effeminate. John Bull, by contrast, is represented as 'an honest plain-dealing Fellow, Cholerick, Bold and of a very unconstant Temper. . . . John was quick, and understood his business very well, but no Man alive was more careless in looking into his Accounts, or more cheated by Partners, Apprentices, and Servants: This was occasioned by his being a boon-Companion, loving his Bottle and his Diversion.'[2]

Arbuthnot's satire hit home and over the next forty years John Bull entered the culture as the personification of the active, quarrelsome, simple-minded English people. He was particularly popular with Arbuthnot's fellow Scots. Both David Hume and Tobias Smollett made elaborate use of him, and by the 1780s James Boswell found it natural to describe Dr Johnson as a 'John Bull' or at least a 'John Bull *philosophe*'.[*3]

Despite Bull's early literary career, however, it was graphic artists who did most to turn him into the famous figure he later became. In the course of the eighteenth century, there had emerged in England a

*And not without good cause. There was something positively Bullish in Johnson's prejudice against foreigners, robust plain speech, respect for common sense, taste for tavern life, disregard for dress, disapproval of over-refinement, especially in cooking, and appetite for red meat. 'I never knew a man', Boswell recorded, 'who relished eating more than Dr Johnson did. When at table he was totally absorbed in the business of the moment; . . . nor would he, unless when in very high company, say one word, or even pay the least attention to what was said by others, till he had satisfied his appetite: which was so fierce, and indulged with such intenseness, that while in the act of eating, the veins of his forehead swelled, and generally a strong perspiration was visible. . . . He was [once] so much displeased with the performance of a nobleman's French cook, that he exclaimed with vehemence, "I'd throw such a rascal into the river"' (pp. 290–91, Dent).

vibrant satirical print culture, one partly created, partly exploited, by Hogarth. From the last decades of the eighteenth century until the end of the Napoleonic Wars, however, this culture underwent a particularly remarkable flowering, as a number of new West End dealers began to trade in high-priced political caricatures, generally based on first-hand observation from the galleries in the Houses of Parliament.[4]

Many qualities distinguished the new satire from the old. The younger generation, led by Thomas Rowlandson and James Gillray (both born in the mid-1750s), pioneered new techniques. In place of the small, heavily crosshatched, black and white engravings of their predecessors, they created larger, lighter etchings, with great economy of line and bright, delicate, hand-filled colour. Where pictorial satire had traditionally relied heavily on the use of visual emblems to make its point – a boot for the Scottish Prime Minister Bute, a fox for Charles James Fox, a crown for the king – the new caricature was simpler and freer and offered lifelike depictions of political actors. Finally, Rowlandson, Gillray and their colleagues were much more daring than their predecessors. Rowlandson's images were often sexually extremely explicit, if not quite pornographic – he was too detached an observer of human lust and vanity to count as a pornographer. Gillray was only too happy to depict Prime Minister Pitt riding naked on a horse, with an evil demon clinging to his back.*

*Foreign travellers were astounded by the way in which English cartoonists were allowed to pillory politicians, aristocrats and royalty. One German visitor found it almost incredible that Gillray was permitted to produce and display his satires on the king and queen and leading government ministers around the corner from the royal palace, 'on the spot which they frequently passed twenty times on their morning walk' (Archenholz, quoted Diana Donald, *The Age of Caricature* (Yale, 1996) p. 2). Here was evidence that the British really were freer than other peoples.

The work of Rowlandson, Gillray and their generation would have stood out in any circumstances. They broke the mould. But these artists were inevitably sucked into the controversy stoked by the French Revolution and the Revolutionary Wars; it gave their work an added intensity. English public opinion initially tended to welcome the French Revolution, which it interpreted, on the model of their own revolution of 1688, as securing the French people basic rights against an absolutist king. One curious and relatively crude cartoon captures this interpretation in the language of roast beef. *Revolution, or Johnny Bull in France* depicts a bull, representing both John Bull and Revolution, tossing Marie Antoinette, often thought to be the real power behind the French king, in the air. Meanwhile the French army looks on approvingly, chanting *The Roast Beef of Old England*. On closer

W. Dent, *Revolution, or Johnny Bull in France*, 1789

examination, the French soldiers prove to be constructed out of roast beef, plum pudding and tankards of ale – dividends that, the print's creator suggests, an English form of government can be expected to deliver.

With the abolition of the French monarchy, however, the execution of the royal family, and the advent of the Terror, public opinion slowly formed into two opposing camps, identified with the conservative Edmund Burke on the one hand and the radical Tom Paine on the other. Conservatives accused radicals of wanting to overthrow King and Constitution, and, with the outbreak of war with France in 1793, of siding with the enemy. Radicals in turn pointed to the suppression, from 1792, of radical publications as evidence that the British government was intent on imposing its own 'Reign of Terror'. Later, parliamentary Acts against sedition and public meeting, coupled with the growing threats of French invasion – from 1798 to 1805 the conquest of Britain was Napoleon's primary strategic aim – weakened the radical cause and drove what was left of it underground. This was a period of extreme, at times hysterical Gallophobia; royalist propaganda typically depicted France as a hellish inferno populated by cannibals – a land, in the words of one Rowlandson print, of 'ATHEISM, PERJURY, REBELLION, TREASON, ANARCHY, MURDER, EQUALITY, MADNESS, CRUELTY, INJUSTICE, TREACHERY, INGRATITUDE, IDLENESS, FAMINE, NATIONAL AND PRIVATE RUIN, *MISERY*' (*The Contrast*, 1792). As the war ended, however, and hundreds of thousands of disaffected troops were demobilised to face unemployment and inflation, so radicalism found its voice again, with mass petitions for electoral reform and violent demonstrations against high prices.

The French Revolution, in other words, inaugurated an extraordinarily impassioned war of values, ideas and images, and the satirical print was naturally deployed by both sides – most cartoonists, including Rowlandson and Gillray (at least in the first half of his career), took commissions from government and opposition parties alike. Hundreds of cartoons alternatively demonising Napoleon and his supporters or (less frequently) Pitt and his, poured from the presses every month, along with sermons, squibs, treatises and counter treatises. In the absence of photography, it was cartoonists who did most to fix images of the English and the French leaders – Pitt and Fox, Robespierre and Napoleon – in the nation's mind. Indeed, the satirists' work in these years was not only reproduced in loose prints, broadsides and ballad sheets but on crockery, coins and handkerchiefs as well. Many a patriot poured his ale from a jug depicting the heart-wrenching scene as Louis XVI said farewell to his family before his execution, or served his plum pudding from a bowl contrasting the happy condition of the beef-eating Briton with the predicament of the root-chewing French slave.

John Bull was, in fact slow to be taken up by visual artists. He had forerunners in the archetypal figures of the English sailor, Jack Tar, or the London butcher, and cows or bulls were sometimes used as a symbol of England or the English. But it was fifty years after Arbuthnot's allegory that John Bull first made an explicit appearance in a print, and this, ironically enough given John Bull's popularity with Scottish writers, was in an anti-Scottish cartoon of the 1760s, showing Bull, a miserable wretch, straining under the weight of his freeloading Scottish sister, Peg.

Other prints, however, quickly followed, and Bull soon came to absorb older figures, including the butcher and the sailor, as the archetypal Englishman. John Bull is the star of some five hundred prints from the Revolutionary period (1789–1815) in the British Museum alone, outstripping George III, the Prince Regent, Pitt,

Anon., ***A Poor Man Loaded with Mischief, or John Bull and his sister Peg,*** **1762**

Nelson, Wellington, and even 'Boney' (Napoleon).

Given their huge number, it was only natural that the Bull prints should represent him in many different guises and put him to many different uses. He could appear as a bull, bulldog or bull man, as well as a man, and was cast not only as a farmer – his usual occupation – but as a sailor, artisan and merchant. Sometimes he was even equated with Charles James Fox or George III. Nevertheless, certain characteristics and attitudes tend to mark him out. First, Bull was firmly associated with roast beef and bulldogs. Again and again he is shown, as in Gillray's *Politeness,* a marvellously vivid etching of 1779 (reproduced on the cover of this book), gorging on beef, plum pudding and ale, mastiff at his side. And generally, although this is not true of Gillray's print, his figure and face are ruddy and bullish. Once

J. Aiken, *Billy's Hobby-horse, or John Bull Loaded with Mischief*, 1795

again, moreover, there was almost always a contrast, explicit or implied, with Bull's opposite, the thin, vain, scheming Frenchman.*

Secondly, Bull was generally represented as a subject, as distinct

* Beef remained, in the last quarter of the eighteenth century, a popular patriotic symbol – the John Bull prints were drawing on its continued significance. One Bristol procession in honour of a naval victory of 1782 included:

> A fine jolly fellow whose countenance and corpulence rendered him highly proper to represent the character of an Englishman, with a fine piece of roast beef on a staff, and for his companion he had a Frenchman, whose meagre visage, voracious glances at the sirloin, and characteristic dress, could not have been surpassed by the pencil of Hogarth.

(*Bristol Journal*, 16 November 1782, quoted in Linda Colley, 'Radical Patriotism in Eighteenth-century England', in *Patriotism, The Making . . . of British National Identity*, ed. Raphael Samuel, London, 1989, p. 171). A decade later, a procession of five or six thousand radical patriots in Sheffield drew a roasted ox through the streets amid the firing of canon in celebration of French victory at Valmy.

from a citizen; he was not ruler but ruled. This was not always the case. The John Bull of Gillray's *Politeness* appears a close cousin of the butchers of *The Beaux Disaster, The Brentford Election* and other patriotic prints of the 1760s and 1770s. He is a freestanding individual, subservient to none. And there are other examples. But from his birth in Arbuthnot's allegory, Bull was generally presented as a man governed, or, in the worst case, exploited by others. The contrast between the butcher of the pre-Revolutionary period and the Bull of the Revolutionary era is indeed striking, and provides testimony to the change wrought by the Revolution itself. It was as if, with the French now living under a republic, everyone suddenly saw the English for what they were: not citizens but more or less loyal, more or less well-governed subjects.

If John Bull was generally conceived not as a master but mastered, not a free city dweller but a man of the field, the satirists could, and did, take different attitudes towards this model. On the one hand, he was often used in anti-government prints to criticise high taxes, government corruption, the royal family or censorship. Cartoonists often played, in particular, on Bull's bovine character, displaying him as an ox, loaded down with financial burdens, whipped by cruel masters, or led by a ring through his nose.

At the other extreme, in the conservative prints, John Bull could feature as a moderately contented subject, one wise enough to defer to his social superiors in the knowledge that they knew what was best for him. Much was made of his blessings in terms of roast beef and plum pudding, his anti-intellectualism and instinctive respect for authority – all, again, by way of contrast to the ravenous, cannibalistic Frenchman, mesmerised by high falutin' revolutionary ideas. Another class of pro-government John Bull prints took the form of the cautionary tale and showed Bull dabbling in reform politics, only to

West, ***A Lock'd Jaw for John Bull,*** **1795**

rue the day. Generally, though, Bull hovered ambiguously between these two extremes. The prints tended to depict Bull as unfairly exploited, victimised or duped by his betters, while acknowledging that he remained *relatively* fortunate and free – he was still better off than most Frenchmen. He stood for a public with certain limited, negative rights, but which had little real power over a remote and corrupt government elected on a narrow franchise. If he grudgingly accepted his condition, it was as the best of a bad lot.

One artist, however, stepped out of the frame altogether, and broke with the Bull conventions.

By the time James Gillray died in 1815, a few days before the Battle of Waterloo, he was widely acknowledged at home and abroad as the greatest political caricaturist Europe had yet produced. Little, however, is known about his life. Gillray was born in 1756 or '57, in a tiny cottage in Chelsea, the son of the sexton to Chelsea's Moravian community and the only one of five children to survive into adulthood. His father, from a modest Scottish Calvinist family, had enlisted in the Royal Cavalry as a young man, and lost an arm fighting the French in 1745. It was while living as a Chelsea Pensioner in the Royal Hospital that he joined the Moravian Brotherhood, a long-persecuted, extremely evangelical Protestant sect. The Moravians, originally from Silesia, based their religion on a belief in the corruption of man and the anticipation of death as a release from life's earthly wretchedness. Gillray attended a Moravian boarding school until he was eight, the only formal schooling he is known to have received, and though he does not seem to have developed into a particularly devout man, his Moravian upbringing must have shaped his dark, unforgiving view of humanity – among other tenets, Moravian children were taught to delight in funerals.

Like Hogarth, Gillray was apprenticed to a London engraver, before being admitted to the newly founded Royal Academy to study engraving.[5] It was while there that he began to etch political caricatures, based on regular visits to the galleries of the Houses of Parliament, although at this stage Gillray probably still hoped to set up as an engraver of history paintings, portraits and other polite forms – caricature was just a means to paying the bills. Indeed, early in the 1780s Gillray more or less gave up caricature altogether, trying his hand as a painter instead. It is not clear what drew him back to satire, but it is certain that he was now able to bring a painter's experience to the form. Gillray was a master craftsman, continuously experimenting with new printing techniques to get the lines, shadings and grains he wanted. But part of his genius as a graphic artist lay in the way he both absorbed and parodied the language of high art; his greatest prints have the delicacy of line, complexity of form, close psychological observation and high drama of great painting. All used, of course, to grotesque, satirical effect.

As a young man, Gillray had a reputation for loose living, and his early satires, although showing signs of his talent, are comparatively crude and aimless. In 1791, however, two years after the beginning of the French Revolution, he settled down to etch more or less exclusively for a print seller, Hannah Humphrey, younger sister of his first publisher. With Gillray's aid, Hannah Humphrey rose to become one of London's leading print sellers, finally moving to an elegant shop on St James's. She in turn looked after Gillray, providing him with a studio and living quarters above her shop. These conditions seem to have suited him well. By the end of the 1790s, the posting of a new Gillray print in Mrs Humphrey's St James's Street window – he produced one every week or so – had become something of a London event, guaranteed to draw a crowd.

Gillray, although generally quiet and reserved, was given to bouts of manic enthusiasm – he was often 'hyped up'. Indeed, at least one man who knew him well, the young cartoonist George Cruikshank, the closest Gillray had to an artistic heir, found the key to Gillray's work in his unbalanced mental state, suggesting 'the bold and vigorous style of Gillray's designs and etchings was entirely owing to the degree of enthusiasm he brought to bear . . . indeed, to a pitch painful to witness, as it exhibited a mind touched with madness'.[6] In 1810 he collapsed into insanity, dying five years later.

Gillray's politics remain something of an enigma. He showed radical sympathies when young, and like many Britons initially welcomed the French Revolution – one early, unlikely 'Contrast' print, *France Freedom, Britain Slavery* (1789), goes so far as to reverse all the old stereotypes and juxtaposes the French, newly liberated from absolutism, and the English, enslaved by the Prime Minister Pitt and his high taxes. By the mid-1790s, however, Gillray was taking regular commissions for George Canning, Pitt's chief propagandist, and by 1797 was in receipt of a government pension. Gillray himself spoke cynically about his change of view: 'Now the Opposition are poor, they do not buy my prints and I must draw on the purses of the larger parties.' But this was almost certainly a pose. There is every reason to believe that Gillray was, like many of his pious, traditionally minded compatriots, revolted by the excesses of the Revolution in France; by what he saw as its mindless persecution of clergy and aristocracy, and its taste for war; by its facile belief in progress and reason and the goodness of man.

Most of Gillray's most memorable prints of the next two decades were thus devoted to the anti-Revolutionary cause; at their best they are extraordinarily dark and disturbing things. Many caricaturists depicted the beheading of Louis XVI, but none matched the chilling intensity of Gillray's *The Blood of the Murdered Crying Out for Vengeance*, which showed the king's head, sliced from his body and lying on the floor, his last, eloquent (and entirely fictitious) words of vengeance, floating away in a cloud of bloody vapour above him. Again, other satirists had fun adapting old images of the Frenchman to the portrayal of the new figure of the revolutionary sans culotte, but Gillray's sarcastically entitled *The Zenith of French Glory; – The Pinnacle of Liberty* outdid them all. It is, in fact, another print portraying the execution of Louis XVI, but this time Gillray has given pride of place not to the king but to an unforgettable image of a bare-arsed Revolutionary spectator, joyously fiddling away above the swinging bodies of three murdered clergymen. His skinny frame and ponytail, the elegant little knives thrust in his belt and daintily poised violin,

The Zenith of French Glory: _ The Pinnacle of Liberty.
Religion, Justice, Loyalty, & all the Bugbears of Unenlighten'd Minds, Farewell!

James Gillray, *The Zenith of French Glory*, 1793

identify him as a close relative of Hogarth's mincing French dancing masters and fencing tutors. But if Gillray's sans culotte is half-French Fribble, he is also half-devil.

These cartoons capture, like nothing else, the character of the anti-French patriotism of these years. Yet it is important to appreciate that Gillray was much more than just a government propagandist. For there is a sense in which his satire was unpartisan. It spared no one. Even Pitt, for whom Gillray sometimes worked more or less directly, was often included within his aim. *Light Expelling Darkness,* a painting in Gillray's best mock-heroic style, represents Pitt as a muscular Apollo, in a chariot drawn by the British lion, scattering the evil spirits of the opposition Whigs before him. Yet the print works less as a glorification of Pitt than as a satire on government attempts to glorify him – and on the exaggerated terms in which it denigrates the radical opposition.

Indeed, like other paintings in Gillray's 'grand' manner, *Light Expelling Darkness* does not just seem to satirise the subject at hand, but the very possibility of human heroism – even human virtue. Writing nine years after Gillray's death, his friend Henry Angelo reflected that the great caricaturist 'seemed scarcely to think at all and to care no more for the actors in the mighty drama which he depicted, nor for the events which he so wonderfully dramatised, than if he had no participation in the good or evil of his day'. But this was not quite right. Gillray was disdainful, not indifferent. A cosmic disillusion runs through his art.

These aspects of Gillray's work – his deep conservatism and his even deeper pessimism – are very much to the fore again in his John Bull prints. Like Rowlandson and other cartoonists of the time, Gillray made much use of John Bull and associated symbols. The print *John Bull taking a Luncheon* (1798), for instance, created shortly after

Nelson's victory over the French at Aboukir Bay – showing a well-heeled Bull, with a massive belly, tree-trunk legs and a large jug of 'True British Stout' by his side, consuming platefuls of French battleships ('frigasees'), handed to him by victorious British admirals – stands foursquare in the tradition of the John Bull print.

Similarly, *Consequences of a Successful French Invasion,* executed a little earlier in the same year, although a much more pessimistic work, makes use of many of the standard John Bull tropes. Enslaved by characteristically overdressed French soldiers, a clog-wearing Bull is put to work in the fields, like a beast of burden. The piles of turnips and onions and cauldron of *soupe maigre* behind him, like the garlic being grown in the fields, stand as stark reminders of the dire culinary consequences of a successful French invasion.

James Gillray, *John Bull taking a Luncheon,* 1798

James Gillray, *Consequences of a Successful French Invasion*, 1798

Indeed perhaps the best-selling print that Gillray ever produced represents another exercise in the same genre. *French Liberty, British Slavery,* like Gillray's earlier work, *Politeness,* draws a starkly simple contrast between the condition of the starving, root-eating Frenchman and the fat, roast beef-eating John Bull. Like Hogarth's *The Gate of Calais,* to which it is in many ways a successor, it was reproduced not only as a print, but on crockery and as a medal as well.

Yet there is something new in these images. For in Gillray's hands, Bull's comic traits are pushed to an extreme. His Bull is only distantly related to the honest, jovial, patriotic Englishman of most Bull prints. Instead he is almost invariably depicted as a grotesquely ugly, moronic, gullible and ungrateful creature, a representative of what Burke contemptuously referred to as the 'swinish multitude', only too ready

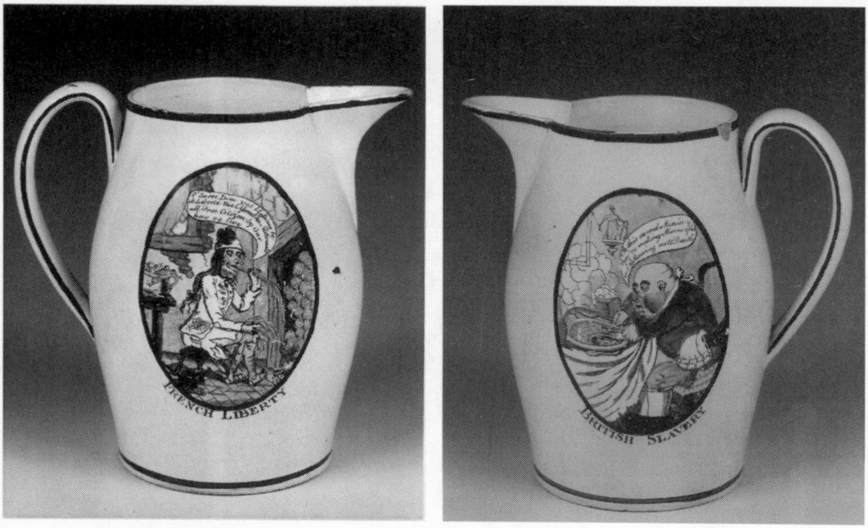

Creamware jug with design from Gillray *'French Liberty, British Slavery'*, *c.*1793

to rise up and massacre its rightful masters. Indeed, Gillray's Bull displays the thick lips, wide nose, and short forehead that the eighteenth-century physiognomy – the science of facial structure – associated with 'negroes' and identified as a sign of retardation. Gillray's John Bull was a black man.[7]

The imagery associated with him is similarly recast. Hogarth's pictures and Fielding's novels abound with low, tavern scenes that work, among other things, as a deliberate riposte to the (alleged) pretentiousness of much high-minded French art. Gillray's prints too, are full of images of people eating and drinking, but these activities have lost their relatively gentle, comic associations. Gillray's subjects don't just feast; they gorge, vomit and shit. In *Un petit Souper à la Parisienne,* a savage parody of Revolutionary propaganda depicting 'le bon sans Culotte' by his fireside, the French no longer eat fricassees but their fellow human beings: sharp-teethed market women dig into a heart and some testicles, while bare-legged sans culottes savour human arms and eyes. In the background, a misshapen hag roasts a baby on a piece of string before an open fire – a primitive substitute for an English roasting jack.

In *Taking Physick*, 1792, George III and his queen sit bare-arsed on two adjoining privies, quite literally scared shitless at the news that the French have killed the Swedish king. Just as Bull is represented, even in *French Liberty, British Slavery,* Gillray's most popular print, as a fat-brained oaf, so the haunch of beef in front of him is depicted as an object of gross, indiscriminate greed.

Gillray might have earned much of his living as a propagandist for the English government, but in his hands John Bull and roast beef

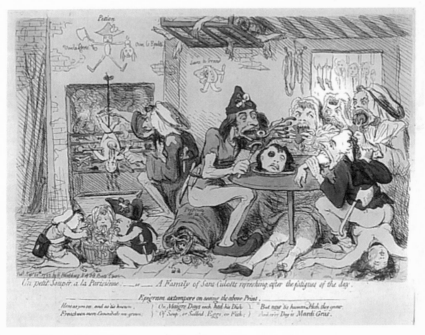

James Gillray, *Un petit Souper a la Parisienne,* 1792

cease to work as positive, patriotic images at all. Instead, they evoke disgust.

Gillray, with his Scottish father and Moravian upbringing, ever the outsider, was like a guest who arrives uninvited to a party and then jeers and heckles the company. This rude intervention did not explode the self-congratulatory cult around roast beef or kill off John Bull, but it represented an early and unforgettable assault on both. Though there would be many more patriotic treatments of these subjects, none would ever have Gillray's power.

11

New World

> I say to you that you are better than a Frenchman. I would lay even money that you who are reading this are more than five feet seven in height, and weigh eleven stone, while a Frenchman is five feet four and does not weigh nine. The Frenchman has after his soup a dish of vegetables, where you have one of meat. You are a different and superior animal – a French-beating animal (the history of a hundred years has shown you to be so).
>
> William Makepeace Thackeray, 1841[1]

WITH THE EMERGENCE of John Bull as prime representative of the male, middle-class, English subject during the French Revolutionary Wars, the final element of England's bovine symbolic network fell firmly in place. But that does not mean the history of these symbols had come to an end. Far from it.

The Victorians consumed vast quantities of beef, much of it transported round the country by the new-fangled railway. Wakefield cattle market, which sold 5,527 head of cattle in 1805, sold 73,456 in 1901, and this scale of increase was not untypical.[2] As the undisputed national dish, the consumption of roast beef remained the favourite way of marking public holidays, local fairs and other special occasions. In October 1844, the overseers of St Luke's Workhouse,

Middlesex, ordered that its inmates be given a dinner of roast beef and ale to celebrate the opening of the royal exchange.[3] After her daughter Emily's wedding at Charlecote, Warwickshire, on 21 October 1845, Mary Elizabeth Lucy, lady of the manor, recorded in her memoirs: 'At three o'clock every cottage on the estate was regaled with beef, plum pudding and good ale in the new loft over the stables which holds about 300. At nine o'clock the tenantry, their wives and sons and daughters began to arrive for a ball.'[4] Queen Victoria's golden and diamond jubilees were celebrated by many an ox roast and as late as 1911 eight cattle and seven pigs were roasted at Stratford-upon-Avon's annual 'mop', or job, fair.[5]

Turkey, it is true, became an increasingly popular Christmas dish at

George Cruikshank, *Roast Oxen for birthday celebrations of John Pole*, 1829. Two massive oxen, complete with gilded horns, being roasted in celebration of the twenty-first birthday of John Pole of Shute Barton.

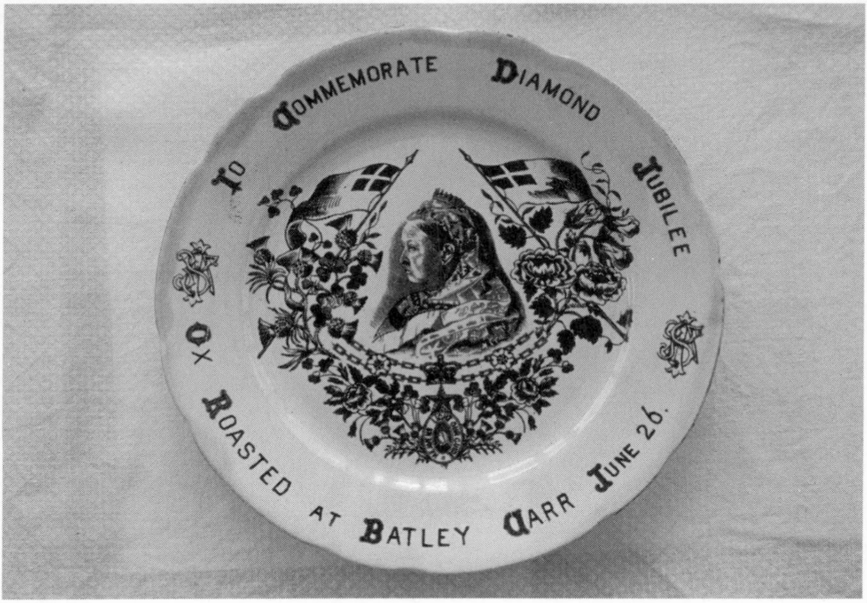

Commemorative plate of the Ox Roast at Batley Carr, 1898

least with those upper- and middle-class households which could afford it. Beef, however, traditional Christmas fare, was still widely served, and given out to the workers and the poor. The Liberal politician and historian, Otto Trevelyan, who inherited Wallington in Northumberland in 1886, gave out 'Xmas beef' to his employees every year, the portions being four pounds for a single man, six pounds for a man and wife and one pound for every child.[6] Up in London, the purchase of 'Christmas beef' from the stalls or shops that sprung up around Smithfield cattle show, which by 1850 had moved from Smithfield to the more elegant Baker Street, became part of the metropolitan Christmas ritual.[7]

Beef was eaten more regularly in the upmarket restaurants, hotels and gentlemen's clubs that sprang up across the country in the course of the nineteenth century. Stendhal, who visited England in the 1820s, staying at the Tavistock Hotel in Covent Garden, a place 'for well-to-do provincials visiting London', recalled that 'one lunched in a dining room which appeared to me about a hundred foot long, thirty wide and twenty high'.

> There you ate everything you wanted and as much as you wanted for fifty sous. They made you an infinity of beefsteaks or placed before you a haunch of roast beef weighing forty pounds and a very sharp knife. Then came the tea to stew all this meat. The dining room opened on to the arcades of Covent Garden. Every morning I saw about thirty good Englishmen gravely walking there, many of them looking unhappy. There was about them no noisy French affection or foppishness.[8]

The best gentlemen's clubs employed French chefs – including, in Louis Eustache Ude and Alexis Soyer, some of the greatest of their day. In this way, they spread an appreciation of French cooking. But roast meat of one sort or another, cooked on gleaming, weight-operated, jack racks, remained a fixed feature of their menus, adding to the peculiarly English character of these institutions.

At home, too, meals tended to centre on beef and mutton, despite technological developments that might have been expected to open up new culinary avenues.* There were reasons for this. The Victorians took a dim view of vegetables, especially salads, which they believed had no nutritional value and fermented in the stomach.

* The steam engine, the glasshouse, new preservative techniques and other innovations both lowered the cost of food and increased its variety. Mrs Beeton's cookbook of 1861 took it for granted that housewives could easily find coriander seed, chillies, peaches and pineapples. The evolution of the multi-purpose coal range at the end of the eighteenth century, and then the gas oven towards the end of the nineteenth, made cooking easier.

The Smithfield Club Show, *Illustrated London News*, 1851. A visit to The Smithfield Club cattle show was a popular London Christmas treat.

They associated onions, garlic, leeks and mushrooms – 'toadstools' – with smelly Frenchmen, pulses with animals, grains with the poor. One guide to female conduct declared the smell of onions to be quite intolerable: 'The loveliest mouth in the world would have no charm if instead of a pure breath . . . it emitted a pungent odour of onions, garlic, chalot, or any such horror.'[9] Poultry and game (the marketing of the latter was only legalised in 1831) remained expensive, which left the cow, the sheep, and to a lesser extent, pigs and fish, as staples. And as in the eighteenth century, meat was still predominantly boiled or roasted – the English never developed the art of braising or stewing – with preference going to roasting.[*10]

Even with the rise of the multi-purpose coal range, open fire roasting in particular remained a peculiar feature of the English domestic kitchen. Ranges meant that fires became smaller and so horizontal spits gave way to vertical ones. This resulted in the evolution of a new lighter species of 'bottle' jack, operated by a coiled spring that had to be wound up like a clock. The steady tick of the bottle jack, as its flywheel rotated, first one way and then the other, was a familiar sound in Victorian kitchens, though sometimes in poorer houses a piece of string, wound up and then left to unwind, had to suffice. According to one oral report, a household in Bedminster, Bristol, relied on a 'skein of black wool' to turn the meat until around 1930. Then a bottle jack was purchased which was used until 1946, when a gas cooker was at last acquired.[11] Poorer families might only cook a roast on a Sunday. Ways, then, had to be found of using up the remainders throughout the rest of the week in the form

* 'The real art of stewing is almost unknown in Great Britain and even in Ireland, despite the fame of the "Irish Stew". Everything that is not roasted or fried is boiled at "a gallop" . . . Such a thing as a stewpan is almost unknown in houses supported by less than three to five hundred a year.' W.H. Wills, 'A Good Plain Cook', *Household Words,* Vol I, 5, p. 138.

of a dispiriting regimen of cold cuts, shepherd's pies, hashes, rissoles and the like, enlivened (if that is the right word) by instant gravies and bottled sauces. By a process that still remains obscure, English cooking thus lost much of its zest. The reliance on fresh, robust ingredients, simply prepared, became, at least in many urban homes, a memory. Writing in Dickens' weekly journal *Household Words* in 1850, W.H. Wills noted that, unlike their equivalents on the Continent, middle-class English women were taught to look down on cookery as a subject unworthy of their attention: 'it is never discussed otherwise than apologetically with a simpering sort of jocularity, or as something which it is low to know anything about. . . . People in best society do not hesitate to bore others with their ailments, or talk about cures and physic; but conversation respecting prevention and wholesomely prepared food is tabooed.'[12] Foreigners began to observe, truly, that if the English had some of the best produce in the world, they also had some of the worst food.

The development of prize breeds added a new element to the old beef cult. Principles of selective breeding had been understood and used by racehorse owners in Stuart times. But they did not begin to be applied to other species of livestock in any systematic way until the 1740s, when the wealthy Leicestershire landowner, Robert Bakewell, began a series of experiments that had, by the 1770s, produced much improved breeds of quick-fattening 'New Leicester' sheep and 'New Longhorn' cows. Thereafter the promotion of select breeding became a fashionable patriotic cause and quickly transformed the quality of the nation's livestock; the average weight of cattle and sheep sold at Smithfield doubled between 1710 and 1795.[13] Leading agricultural 'improvers', like the Duke of Bedford and Thomas Coke (later Lord Leicester), held open days at their farms, giving the public the chance to admire their enhanced animals, model buildings and revolutionary farming techniques; in addition they clubbed together to form societies devoted to propagandising 'the best and most profitable breeds of sheep and cattle'. By 1803 there were at least thirty-two local agricultural societies in existence, all of which had their own annual shows, London's Smithfield Christmas show being only the most prestigious. As with today's agricultural shows, these featured livestock competitions and showcased new commodities and services. They also offered breeders the chance to display celebrated exhibition animals, like the 'Durham Ox', the 'Craven Heifer', the 'White Heifer' and the 'Famous Lincolnshire Ox' – castrated males which had been bred and then fattened to reach gargantuan sizes. The Durham Ox, the prototype for

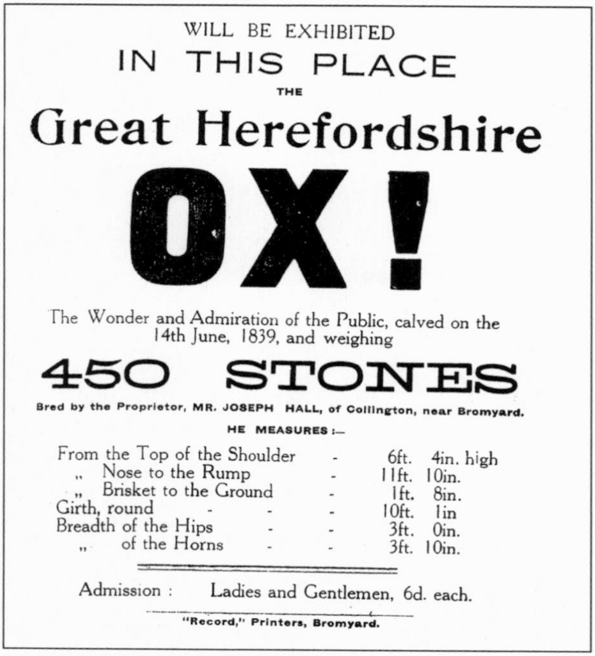

WILL BE EXHIBITED

IN THIS PLACE

THE

Great Herefordshire

OX!

The Wonder and Admiration of the Public, calved on the 14th June, 1839, and weighing

450 STONES

Bred by the Proprietor, MR. JOSEPH HALL, of Collington, near Bromyard.

HE MEASURES :—

From the Top of the Shoulder	-	6ft.	4in. high
„ Nose to the Rump	-	11ft.	10in.
„ Brisket to the Ground	-	1ft.	8in.
Girth, round - -	-	10ft.	1in
Breadth of the Hips -	-	3ft.	0in.
„ of the Horns -	-	3ft.	10in.

Admission : Ladies and Gentlemen, 6d. each.

"Record," Printers, Bromyard.

Bill advertising the Great Herefordshire Ox, 1844

the others and, like most of them, the work of two pioneer breeders, the Colling brothers, was said to have stood five feet six inches tall and weigh 3,204 pounds. Bought by an enterprising publicist, John Day, it crisscrossed the country from London to Edinburgh in a specially built carriage, being exhibited, between 1801 and 1807, in two hundred venues. In 1802 he spent nearly a year in London where takings on one day alone amounted to £97.[14]

As the aristocratic titles ranged above suggest, select breeding was an expensive pursuit, enjoyed mainly by rich landowners, and some historians have argued that it worked as a subtle ideological

James Pollard, *The Butcher's Shop*, 1822. 'Traceability', nineteenth-century fashion. The meat on display includes prize-winning beasts from the Smithfield show.

affirmation of aristocratic values of good breeding and conspicuous display over usefulness.[15] (As critics pointed out at the time, the largest, most acclaimed beasts were poor breeders and produced overly fatty butcher's meat.) Perhaps so, but the improved animals were popular not just with the landowners but with the crowds who flocked in their thousands to agricultural shows across the country. Pubs were named after the most famous animals and butchers paid considerable sums for joints of meat from them. These were proudly displayed in their windows before being sold off to valued customers or donated to public dinners.

Prize cattle, their genealogy carefully recorded in 'herd books', the farmyard counterpart of *Debrett*'s, generated a new, characteristically British artistic genre: livestock portraiture. In an age before the camera, livestock breeders turned to painters for a visual record of their marvellous creations. Again, it was racehorses which first set the pace, and the greatest of the livestock portraitists, George Stubbs, continued to specialise in horses. But other artists, including Thomas Weaver and George Garrard, produced lovingly exact images of prize-winning cattle in all their proud, fatty British stateliness. And these images, like the animals themselves, were enjoyed not just by their owners, but by the nation at large. Many agricultural periodicals offered engraved animal portraits, suitable for framing – more than two thousand prints of the Durham Ox were sold in 1802 alone. Many John Bulls must have digested their beef and pudding while gazing at them.

With the development of spectacularly improved Scottish Highland, Shorthorn, Galloway and Aberdeen Angus breeds in the early nineteenth century, Scotland, so long the butt of English kitchen chauvinism, was at last allowed to join the party. The roast beef of old England, much of which had, in truth, always originated north of the

Patriot, after Thomas Weaver, 1804. Meat from improved cattle was often, by our standards, excessively fatty – the meat from the great prize-winning specimens especially so. On the other hand, nineteenth-century cattle were reared on a diet rich in flowers and herbs, and their meat would have had more flavour than that from cattle reared on chemically blitzed grass and factory feed.

border, now became 'the Roast Beef of Old Britain'. The survival, to this day, of the Aberdeen and Angus steakhouse chains – still with their ersatz velvet seats and ruby-coloured walls, distantly Victorian in style – have their origins in the unexpected reversal in the reputation of Scotland's meat.

Indeed, like a super-fit gene, the old yeoman style of English cooking spread not just to Scotland, but across the world. Where the English language went, English culinary techniques and tastes went too. England's Southern and Northern American colonies were founded under very different circumstances and developed distinct economies and cultures – the South slave owning, loose knit and Anglican, the North agrarian, close knit and Puritan. But both identified with (rather different versions of) the patriotic independent English cultivator and his food – Washington and Jefferson were proud farmers. Indeed, until the appearance of Amelia Simmons's *American Cookery* of 1796, American cooks had to make do with pirated editions of 'plain' English books, most notably Eliza Smith's *The Compleat Housewife*, the first cookbook published in America, in 1742, and Susannah Carter's *The Frugal Housewife* (American edition, 1772). New England's reputation for boiled dinners, baked beans ('pease' in seventeenth-century parlance) and pies has its roots in English traditions. But so does the South's Virginia ham and pecan pie. Despite the alien climate, rich planters of the South tended, in fact, to consume more red meat than did their Puritan northern neighbours. The diary of the Virginian gentleman William Byrd shows that he ate beef twenty-four times, between December 1709 and March 1710, pork five times and mutton three – turkey, indigenous to America, he ate only once.[16] Even Jefferson, sometimes criticised by his political opponents for liking Gallic dishes, preferred 'good beef, mutton and lamb' to any other kind of meat.[17]

Even today, despite the long ascendancy of French food among the fashionable, the influence of successive generations of non-English immigrants and the emergence of native tastes and traditions, American cooking retains a recognisable 'plain' English strain. This is especially true among well-born New Englanders, known in the nineteenth century as the 'Roast Beef Bostons'. The food writer Julia Child, who grew up in southern California but whose mother came from good Massachusetts stock, recalled: 'we ate in typically middle-class, WASP American way of the teens and twenties – a big prime-rib roast of beef for the traditional Sunday family lunch of twelve or fourteen people. If not beef, we might have a fine big, well-aged leg of lamb . . . always served with mint sauce as well as gravy.'[18]

And what was true of the USA was even more so of Australia and New Zealand, where colonists, with less exposure to other Western food cultures than their American counterparts, continued, well into the twentieth century, to cook much as Britons did at home. New Zealanders in particular still take a positively eighteenth-century pride in the quality of their roast meat.

Not only did roast beef continue to be eaten in nineteenth-century Britain, it remained an important national symbol. Just as the radicals of the 1760s invoked it to signify the proper birthright of every Englishman, so the Chartists of the 1820s and 1830s, agitating for the abolition of the Corn Laws and parliamentary reform, resorted to the language of roast beef: 'Here's that we may live to see the restoration of old English Times, old English fare, old English holidays and old English justice and everyman live by the sweat of his brow!' extolled Feargus O'Connor, the Chartist leader. And unless anyone doubted what the radicals meant by 'old English fare', they were explicit about it; it was 'a flitch of bacon' or, alternatively, roast beef and plum pudding – the bacon and beef both coming from the animals that, in days of old, villagers were allowed to feed on the common. One Towbridge Chartist assured his comrades that victory in their struggle would mean 'plenty of roast beef, plum pudding and beer by working three hours a day'. It is hardly surprising, then, that when leading Chartists McDouall and Collins were released from prison in 1840, they were fêted at a Manchester dinner whose participants feasted on plum pudding with a band playing *The Roast Beef of Old England* in the background.[19]

True, Chartism was the last important radical movement to look back in this way to a golden, agrarian past – to phrase its demands in terms of 'the ancient laws of England' and roast beef. Henceforth socialists would accept cities and machines as facts of life. But roast beef continued to feature, for instance, in Punch cartoons and music hall songs, as an embodiment of the English way of life.

The nineteenth-century history of roast beef was mirrored by that of the bulldog.

By the early 1800s the identification of animal baiting as the quintessentially English sport was on the decline. It was overshadowed by other games – football, cricket, and above all pugilism or boxing, celebrated in a famous book, *Boxiana,* by the early nineteenth-century journalist Pierce Egan. The real blow, however, came in 1835, when, after a long campaign, baiting with dogs was finally made illegal on the grounds of its cruelty and general roughness.

This, though, did not spell the end of the English bulldog. After a period when the animal, long the most common dog in England, came close to extinction, it re-emerged the object of a very different sort of pastime: dog breeding and dog showing.[20]

The earliest dog shows, around the time of the Revolutionary wars, were informal, plebeian affairs that often took place in pubs – they consisted of little more than a few fanciers gathering together to show off their dogs, arrange matings and debate the proper attributes of the breed. But in the course of the nineteenth century, dog fancying was gradually appropriated by middle-class pet owners, enamoured with the new, biologically dubious notion of 'breeds'. The first formal dog show was held in Birmingham in 1859, and they spread like fleas from there. The Kennel Club was set up fourteen years later, and the first book of pedigrees published in the 1870s. Bulldogs were not by any means the first 'breed' to be taken up by the pedigree-sensitive fancier – they were too closely associated with the lower classes. But, after the launch of the Bulldog Club in 1874, they underwent a rapid rehabilitation, and by 1885 were second only to collies in popularity, as measured by dog show entries.[21] Granted, the bulldog as canonised by the Bulldog Club and still with us today, with its shortened muzzle, receding jaw and miniature legs, looked very different from the fighting dog of old. As one Victorian old-timer complained, 'the disgusting abortions exhibited at the shows [were] deformities from foot to muzzle . . . and totally incapable of coping with a veteran bull'.[22] But the breed's success with fanciers ever since – like its popularity with skinheads, and other tough, chauvinistic types – has much to do with its long identity as the quintessentially English breed, brave, stubborn and carnivorous.

After the butcher – largely eclipsed by John Bull during the period of the Revolutionary Wars – Bull himself proved perhaps the least resilient of the bovine symbols. The Victorian John Bull tends to appear self-satisfied, moralistic and somehow unreal, especially when contrasted with Gillray's glowering figure. The great English historian G.M. Trevelyan once suggested that a Bull of the 1830s, created by the cartoonist John Doyle, was 'perhaps his last entirely satisfactory appearance in art'.[23] Even so, he remained an immensely popular figure with cartoonists, journalists and nationalists, as well as manufacturers wanting to appeal to consumers' patriotic sentiments. John Bull and his bulldog were used to sell Worcester sauce, baking powder, Beechams pills, light bulbs, ginger beer, cocoa powder, bicycles, mustard, lung tonic, Sunlight soap, tobacco, metal polish, beer, croquet, cotton wool, dog cakes and aerated table water, among other things.

*

I have been placing the emphasis on continuity, tracing the way in which the symbols this book is about lived into the nineteenth century and beyond. There is a danger here of exaggeration. By the end of the Victorian era, after all, the world in which roast beef, the bulldog and John Bull came of age had changed almost beyond recognition. These had emerged as symbols of manly patriotism, defined against France abroad and a corrupt cosmopolitan ruling class at home. But the French, while much derided, ceased to figure as an important opponent – the two countries never took opposing sides in a major war after 1817 – while Britain's new enemies, first Protestant Germany and then communist Russia, could hardly be squeezed into the French mould. Back at home, a slow process of reform – the extension of the franchise, the abolition of the tariffs on corn, restrictions on patronage and the sale of public office – effectively destroyed the old regime from within. The English middle classes could no longer be represented as victims of a corrupt social order.

These developments, moreover, were accompanied by others even more profound. It would not be right to say that England's patriotic bovine symbols belonged exclusively to the country rather than the town. Roasting jacks were used in big cities as well as farms. Bull baits were staged at Smithfield as well as in wheat fields. But they found their home in a predominantly agrarian world of independent farmers and artisans, butchers and bakers, a world in which the English really did eat a lot more beef than any of their neighbours, and fierce bulldogs were ubiquitous. As the old agrarian economy gave way to its industrial successor, however, and England became one of the most heavily urbanised societies in the world, so the old bovine symbols became anachronistic. As Trevelyan said of John Bull, 'Since the typical Englishman ceased to be a rustic and became a townee, the stereotypical figure of the stout man in the conventional top hat hardly seems to represent the nation in any convincing manner.'[24] The English now eat a lot more curry than roast beef.

If what I am suggesting is right – if the world in which these symbols had their home has largely ceased to exist – it is hardly surprising if the symbols themselves have lost their power. But the surprising thing is the extent to which they are still alive today. While working on this book, I have built up a thick file of newspaper clippings. They include columns alerting readers to German plans to persuade the European Community to ban the bulldog; accounts of restaurant owners refusing to serve French beef; and the letters to papers lambasting filthy French food. Looking through the file, I see that patriots dressed as John Bull have taken to the streets to voice opposition to the sale of the car manufacturer Rover to a venture capital firm, to Britain joining the Euro, and to the appointment of a Swede to manage the English football team. Photographs show a Tory councillor from Essex parading a bull terrier in a Union Jack waistcoat in protest at the council's refusal to fly a Union Jack, and another of a bulldog that had been used by Pro-Gilbraltar protesters outside the Spanish embassy in London. These symbols might have lost much of their connection with the real world, but, as is so common in Britain, we cling on to them regardless. And now, just as I am sitting down to finish this chapter – and just as France has failed to qualify for the second round of the 2002 World Cup – a letter appears in the *Daily Telegraph*:

> Sir, For those of you who are still wondering why the world champions, France, have made such an early exit from the competition this year, I have the answer: they have been deprived of British beef for the past four years.[25]

Some memories run deep.

Notes

Introduction

1. Nick Fides, *Meat: A Natural Symbol,* London, 1991, offers a lively exploration of symbolic dimension to meat. I have also drawn on Anne Murcott, 'You Are What You Eat', in *The Food Consumer,* C. Ritson et al., eds, London, 1986, and Julia Twigg, 'Vegetarianism and the Meanings of Meat', in Anne Murcott, ed. *Sociology of Food and Eating,* Aldershot, 1983.
2. Hugh Fearnley-Whittingstall, *The River Cottage Cookbook,* London, 2001; Fergus Henderson, *Nose to Tail Eating, A Kind of British Cooking,* London, 1999.

Chapter 1. Beef eaters

1. For general histories of early English eating habits see J.C. Drummond and Anne Wilbraham, *The Englishman's Food,* London, 1939, revised 1957; C. Anne Wilson, *Food and Drink in Britain,* London, 1973; Sara Paston-Williams, *The Art of Dining, A History of Cooking and Eating,* London, 1993.
2. Conrad Russell, *The Crisis of Parliaments: English History 1509–1660,* Oxford, 1971, p. 7.
3. Quoted in Helen Morris, 'No Kickshaws, Whole Bellyfuls', *Wine and Food,* 78, 1953, p. 97.
4. 'London Journal, 1562', ed. Caroline Barron, Christopher Coleman and Claire Gobbi, *The London Journal,* 9 (2), 1983, pp. 136–52.

5. *A Journey into England in the Year 1598*, trans. from the Latin by Richard Bentley, London, 1957.
6. Quoted in William B. Rye, *England as Seen by Foreigners*, London, 1865, p. 70.
7. *A Voyage to England*, London, 1709, pp. 61–2.
8. I owe this observation to a conversation with Professor Ronald Hutton.
9. R.H. Tawney and Eileen Power, eds, *Tudor Economic Documents*, 3 vols, London, 1924, vol. III, p. 51; Joan Thirsk, *The Agrarian History of England and Wales*, vol. IV, 1500–1640, Cambridge, 1967, pp. 209–10.
10. F.J. Fisher, 'The Development of the London Food Market, 1540–1640', *Economic History*, nd, reprinted in E.M. Carus Wilson,ed., *Essays in Economic History*, London, 1954, vol. 1.
11. Henri Misson, *Memoirs and Observations of Travels over England*, London, 1719, pp. 310–11.
12. *Letters Describing the Character and Customs of the English and French Nations*, London, 1726, pp. 39–40.
13. Thomas Dekker, *The Witch of Edmonton*, Act II, Scene 2.
14. Mildred Campbell, *The English Yeoman Under Elizabeth and the Early Stuarts*, New Haven, 1942, p. 165. Though old, this remains the best study of the yeoman.
15. Quoted Campbell, *English Yeoman*, p. 221.
16. Quoted Campbell, *English Yeoman*, p. 52.
17. Thomas Fuller, *The Holy State*, London, 1642, p. 117.
18. *The Description of England*, ed. George Edelen, Washington, DC, 1968, p. 131.
19. Keith Wrightson, *English Society, 1580–1680*, London, 1982, pp. 37–8.
20. Julian Paget, *The Yeoman of the Guard, 1485–1985*, Poole, Dorset, 1984, p. 35.

Chapter 2. Cooks

1. *An Itinerary*, London, 1617, p. 150.
2. *The English Housewife*, London, 1631, pp. 88–94.
3. J.L. Forster, 'Take One Ox', *Food and Wine*, 1953, p. 78.

4. Quoted in David Eveleigh, 'Put down to a clear bright fire'; The English Tradition of Open-Fire Roasting', *Folk Life*, 29, 1990–91, p. 7. I am extremely indebted to this article, which I have drawn on throughout my account of open-fire roasting.
5. Eveleigh, 'Put down to a clear bright fire', p. 8.
6. Eveleigh, 'Put down to a clear bright fire', p. 10.
7. Eveleigh, 'Put down to a clear bright fire', p. 11.
8 *The Dutch Boare Dissected*, 1665, BMC, 1028.
9. For the history of mustard see Rosamond Man and Robin Weir, *The Compleat Mustard*, London, 1988.
10. *The Closet of Sir Kenelm Digby Knight Opened*, 1669, quoted in Elizabeth David, *Spices, Salt and Aromatics in the English Kitchen*, Harmondsworth, 1970, pp. 73–4.
11. Hanna Glasse, *The Art of Cookery Made Plain and Easy*, London, 1747, p. 25.
12. Henri Misson, *Memoirs and Observations of Travels over England*, London, 1719, p. 315.
13. I am grateful to Laura Mason for sending me her unpublished paper 'Puddings and English Identity', January 2001, on which I have drawn here.
14. *Picture of England*, 2 vols, London, 1789, vol. II, pp. 107–14.
15. *Debate Between the Heralds of France and England*, 1549, in R.H. Tawney and Eileen Power, eds, *Tudor Economic Documents*, 3 vols, London, 1924, vol. III, p. 8.
16. Quoted J.C. Drummond and Anne Wilbraham, *The Englishman's Food*, London, 1939, revised 1957, p. 44.
17. Quoted in Pamela Sambrook, *Country House Brewing in England, 1500–1900*, London, 1996, p. 18.

Chapter 3. Fricassees

1. Barbara Wheaton, *Savouring the Past: The French Kitchen and Table from 1300 to 1789*, New York, 1983, ch. 3.
2. Wheaton, *Savouring the Past*, p. 128; Gilly Lehmann, 'Politics in the Kitchen', *18th-Century Life*, 23, 1999, p. 74.

3. Dr Martin Lister, *A Journey to Paris in the Year 1698*, London, 1699, p. 158; Henri Misson, quoted in *Strange Island: Britain Through Foreign Eyes*, ed. Francesca Wilson, London, 1952, p. 52.
4. J. Nichols, *History and Antiquities of the County of Leicester*, 4 vols, London, 1795–1815, vol. III, pt 2, pp. 592–3.
5. Felicity Heal, *Hospitality in Early Modern England*, Oxford, 1990, p. 116.
6. *Diary of a Country Parson*, ed. John Beresford, Oxford, 1978, entry for 10 June 1784.
7. Both quoted in Robert W. Malcolmson, *Popular Recreations in English Society, 1700–1850*, Cambridge, 1973, pp. 61–5.
8. Jack Goody, *Food and Love: A Cultural History of East and West*, London, 1998, p. 134.
9. On this point, as on many others in this chapter, I am indebted to Stephen Mennell's fine survey, *All Manners of Food, Eating and Taste in England and France from the Middle Ages to the Present*, Urbana and Chicago, 1996.

Chapter 4. Patriots

1. R. Campbell, *The London Tradesman*, London, 1747, pp. 276–7.
2. Barbara Wheaton, *Savouring the Past: The French Kitchen and Table from 1300 to 1789*, p. 163.
3. Gilly Lehmann, 'Politics in the Kitchen', *18th-Century Life*, 23, 1999, p. 73.
4. Lehmann, 'Politics in the Kitchen', p. 79.
5. E.J. Hobsbawm, *Nations and Nationalism since 1780*, London, 1990, p. 1.
6. Linda Colley has emphasised the role played by Protestantism in the development of English and British national identity, *Britons, Forging the Nation 1707–1837*, New Haven, 1992, ch. 1.
7. My account of the development of English national consciousness and 'patriotic' thought in the eighteenth century is indebted to Gerald Newman, *The Rise of English Nationalism* (New York, 1997) as well as to Colley's *Britons*.

8. P.G. Dickson, *The Financial Revolution in England: A Study in the Development of Public Credit*, London, 1967; Isaac Kramnick, *Bolingbroke and His Circle: The Politics of Nostalgia in the Age of Walpole*, Ithaca, NY, 1968, pp. 39–48.
9. Julian Hoppit, *A Land of Liberty: England 1689–1727*, Oxford, 2000, p. 337.
10. Print, BMC, 4785.
11. Colley, *Britons*, p. 89.
12. John Brown, *An Estimate of the Manners and Principles of the Times*, 6th edn, 2 vols, 1757, p. 89.
13. L'Abbé Le Blanc, *Letters on the English and French Nations*, 2 vols, Dublin, 1747, vol. II, p. 5.
14. Boorde, Morison and Dekker are all quoted in Helen Morris, 'No Kickshaws, Whole Bellyfuls', *Wine and Food*, 78, 1953, pp. 96–7.
15. *The Description of England*, ed. George Edelen, Washington, DC, 1968, p. 126.
16. London, 1685, 'Preface', no page number.

Chapter 5. Patriots in the Kitchen

1. *The Spectator*, ed. Donald F. Bond, Oxford, 1967, 4 vols, vol. III, letter 308, 22 February 1712.
2. *The Tatler*, ed. Donald F. Bond, Oxford, 1987, 4 vols, vol. II, letter 148, 21 March 1710.
3. For eighteenth-century ices, see Elizabeth David, *Harvest of the Cold Months*, ed. Jill Norman, London, 1994.
4. For Cheyne see Anita Guerrini, *Obesity and Depression in the Enlightenment: The Life and Times of George Cheyne*, Oklahoma, 2000; and Roy Porter's introduction to Cheyne's *The English Malady*, London, 1991.
5. *English Malady*, p. 51.
6. *English Malady*, p. 49.
7. Jennifer Stead, 'Quizzing Glasse: or Hannah Scrutinized', *Petits Propos Culinaires*, 13, 1983, reprinted as foreword to Hanna Glasse, *The Art of Cookery Made Plain and*

Easy, London, 1995, p. xxvii.

8. Glasse, *The Art of Cookery*, p. ii.
9. J.H. Plumb, *Sir Robert Walpole*, 2 vols, London, 1960, vol. I, pp. 81–91, 272–3.
10. *The Norfolk Congresses*, London, 1728, p. 5. For this pamphlet and for criticisms of the Whig ruling class's taste in food generally see Gilly Lehmann, 'Politics in the Kitchen', *18th-Century Life*, 23, 1999.
11. Romney Sedgwick, 'The Duke of Newcastle's Cook', *History Today*, 5, 1955, p. 311.
12. Sedgwick, 'Duke of Newcastle's Cook', p. 314.
13. Sedgwick, 'Duke of Newcastle's Cook', p. 315.
14. Lehmann, 'Politics in the Kitchen', p. 76.

Chapter 6. Actors

1. For the introduction of Italian opera into England and the controversy it stirred see Eric Walter White, *A History of English Opera*, London, 1983.
2. For the development of farce, the multiple bill and pantomime see Simon Trussler, *The Cambridge Illustrated History of the British Theatre*, Cambridge, 1994, pp. 153–7.
3. L'Abbé Le Blanc, *Letters on the English and French Nations*, 2 vols, Dublin, 1747, vol. II, letter LXXXII.
4. See *Ferdinand Count Fathom, The Reprisal or the Tars of Old England*, London, 1757, p. 6.
5. The play, performed on one night only (29 November 1734) is by Louis de Boissy; for the critical reception see *The Prompter*, 27 December 1734.
6. Le Blanc, *Letters*, vol. II, letter LXXXII.
7. For Fielding's early life and career in the theatre see Jenny Uglow, *Henry Fielding*, London, 1995, ch. 1.
8. For the full history and extra stanzas see Edgar V. Roberts, 'Henry Fielding and Richard Leveridge: Authorship of the "Roast Beef of Old England"',

Huntington Library Quarterly, 27, no. 2, February 1964, pp. 175–81.

9. Robert J. Allen, *The Clubs of Augustan London*, Cambridge, Mass., 1933, pp. 137–41.
10. Mr Victor, *The History of the Theatres of London and Dublin*, 3 vols, London, 1761, vol. I, pp. 152–3.
11. By far the most detailed account of the club is Walter Arnold, *The Life and Death of the Sublime Society of Beefsteaks*, London, 1871.
12. *The History of the Mimes and Pantomimes*, London, 1728, p. 5. For Rich see Paul Sawyer, 'John Rich's Contribution to the London Stage', in Kenneth Richards and Peter Tomson, eds, *The 18th-Century English Stage*, London, 1972.
13. For all this and more see Arnold, *Sublime Society of Beefsteaks, passim.*
14. *Boswell's London Journal, 1762–1763*, ed. Frederick A. Pottle, London, 1966, entry for 7 November 1762.
15. *The Connoisseur*, Issue 29, 6 June 1754.

Chapter 7. Hogarth

1. For Hogarth's life and work see Ronald Paulson, *Hogarth*, Cambridge, 1991; David Bindman, *Hogarth*, London, 1981; and Jenny Uglow, *Hogarth: A Life and a World*, London, 1997.
2. John Ireland, *Hogarth Illustrated*, London, 1791, vol. I, pp. 294–5.
3. See *The Dutch Boare Dissected*, 1665, BMC, 1028.
4. Bindman, *Hogarth*, p. 183.
5. This was on show at a small Tate Britain room devoted to the theme of 'roast beef', 1999–2000.
6. *A Cantata. Taken from a Celebrated Print of the Ingenious Mr Hogarth . . . The Words by a Man of Taste*, London, 1759.

Chapter 8. Bulldogs

1. Johannes Caius, *Of Englishe Dogges*, London, 1576, reprinted Amsterdam, 1969, p. 26.

2. Quoted E.K. Chambers, *The Elizabethan Stage,* 3 vols, Oxford, 1923, vol. II, p. 453.
3. Quoted Chambers, *Elizabethan Stage,* vol. II, p. 454.
4. *Letters Describing the Character and Customs of the English and French Nations,* London, 1726, p. 38.
5. *Boswell's London Journal, 1762–1763,* ed. Frederick A. Pottle, London, 1966, entry for 15 December 1762.
6. Robert W. Malcolmson, *Popular Recreations in English Society, 1700–1850,* Cambridge, 1973, p. 63.
7. Quoted Malcolmson, *Popular Recreations,* p. 66.
8. *Diary of a Country Parson,* ed. John Beresford, Oxford, 1978, entry for 5 September 1759.
9. *Henry V,* Act III, Scene 7.
10 Henri Misson, *Memoirs and Observations of Travels over England,* London, 1719, pp. 24–7.
11. Caius, *Of Englishe Dogges,* pp. 25–6.
12. *The Description of England,* ed. George Edelen, Washington DC, 1968, pp. 340, 344.
13. Quoted in Chambers, *Elizabethan Stage,* vol. II, p. 455.
14. *Essays Moral, Political and Literary,* ed. Eugene Miller, Indianapolis, 1985, p. 323.
15. *Letters Describing the Character and Customs of the English and French Nations,* London, 1726, p. 41.
16. *The Craftsman,* issue of 13 September 1729.

Chapter 9. Butchers

1. For a closer reading of this print see Mark Hallet, *Spectacle of Difference, Graphic Satire in the Age of Hogarth,* New Haven, 1999.
2. Henri Misson, *Memoirs and Observations of Travels over England,* London, 1719, p. 146–7.
3. *Letters Describing the Character and Customs of the English and French Nations,* London, 1726, pp. 38–9.
4. Quoted Diana Donald, *The Age of Caricature, Satirical Prints in the Reign of George III,*

New Haven, 1996, p. 109.
5. *Memoirs and Observations*, p. 305.
6. Jenny Uglow, *Hogarth: A Life and World*, London, 1997, p. 490.
7. For an insightful discussion of this phenomenon, see Diana Donald, *Age of Caricature*, ch. 4.
8. 'A Beau's Sunday Morning Walk', *The British Magazine*, January 1747, pp. 6–11.
9. Quoted Peter Ackroyd, *London: A Biography*, London, 2000, p. 268.
10. For the fight between Broughton and Slack, see Pierce Egan, *Boxiana or Sketches of Ancient and Modern Pugilism*, ed. John Ford, Folio Society, London, 1976 (first published 1813), pp. 30–32.
11. H. Walpole, *Memoirs of the Reign of George III*, London, 1845, vol. 1, p. 89.
12. William Hone, *Everyday Book*, 2 vols, London, 1827, vol. 1, p. 1434.
13. *The Oxford Magazine*, V, 1770, p. 216.
14. Quoted Ackroyd, *London*, p. 268.

Chapter 10. John Bull

1. *Works of Art and Artists in England*, 3 vols, London, 1838, vol. III, pp. 132–3.
2. John Arbuthnot, *The History of John Bull*, ed. Alan Bower and Robert Erickson, Oxford, 1976, p. 9. Discussions of John Bull's career include Hugh Cunningham, 'The Languages of Patriotism, 1750–1914', *History Workshop Journal*, No. 12, 1981; Miles Taylor, 'John Bull and the Iconography of Public Opinion in England, 1712–1929', *Past and Present*, vol. 13, February 1992.
3. For David Hume see *Sister Peg: A Pamphlet Hitherto Unknown*, ed. David Raynor, Oxford, 1976. This pamphlet, published in 1660, was published anonymously, but there are good grounds for attributing it to Hume.
4. See Diana Donald, *The Age of Caricature, Satirical Prints in the Reign of George III*, New Haven, 1996, ch. 1 and throughout for a fuller discussion of the development of the late eighteenth-century print.
5. For Gillray see Richard Godfrey, *James Gillray: The Art of Caricature*, London,

2001.

6. Donald, *Age of Caricature*, p. 40.
7. See Donald, *Age of Caricature*, pp. 180–83, for eighteenth-century theories of physiognomy and their influence on Gillray.

Chapter 11. New World

1. The Thackeray epigraph comes from 'Memorials of Gourmandising', *Fraser's Magazine*, 1841. Quoted by George Orwell, 'Dickens', *Collected Essays*, London, 1961, vol. III, p. 54.
2. Peter Brears, *Traditional Food in Yorkshire*, Edinburgh, 1987, p. 96.
3. *The Times*, 30 October 1844, p. 4.
4. Sara Paston-Williams, *The Art of Dining: A History of Cooking and Eating*, London, 1993, p. 313.
5. A.R. Wright, *British Calendar Customs*, ed. T.E. Jones, London, 1938, pp. 98–9.
6. Paston-Williams, *Art of Dining*, p. 271.
7. See Henry Morely's rhapsody on 'Christmas Beef', *Household Words*, vol. XIII, no. 196, 24 December 1853.
8. Stendhal, *Memoirs of an Egotist*, trans. T.W. Earp, London, 1949, p.67–8.
9. *The Ladies Treasury*, vol. I, 1854, p.239, quoted in Sarah Freeman, *Mutton and Oysters: The Victorians and their Food*, London, 1989, p. 70.
10. For Victorian tastes see Freeman, *Mutton and Oysters* and C. Anne Wilson, ed., *Luncheon, Nuncheon and Other Meals. Eating with the Victorians*, London, 1994.
11. David Eveleigh, 'Put down to a clear bright fire'; The English Tradition of Open-Fire Roasting', *Folk Life* 29, 1990–91, p. 16.
12. W. H. Wills, 'A Good Plain Cook', *Household Words*, vol. I, 5, p. 138. p. 140.
13. G.M. Trevelyan, *Illustrated English Social History*, London, 1964, vol. III, p. 150.
14. For the new breeds and the culture that grew up around them see Elizabeth Moncrieff and Stephen and Iona Joseph, *Farm Animal Portraits*, Woodbridge, 1988; Stephen Hall and Juliet Clutton-Brock, *Two Hundred Years of British Farm*

Lifestock, London, 1989; Harriet Ritvo, *The Animal Estate, The English and Other Creatures in the Victorian Age,* Cambridge, Mass., 1987, ch. 1.

15. Ritvo, *Animal Estate,* p. 52.
16. D.H. Fischer, *Albion's Seed: Four British Folkways in America,* New York, 1989, pp. 349–54.
17. Waverley Root and Richard de Rochemont, *Eating in America, A History,* New York, 1976, p. 95.
18. 'Introduction to the Anniversary Edition', in Julia Child, Louissette Bertholle and Simone Beck, *Mastering the Art of French Cooking,* 40th anniversary edition, New York, 2001, p. vii.
19. Hugh Cunningham, 'Language of Patriotism' in Raphael Samuel, ed., *Patriotism,* vol. 1, p. 69.
20. Edgar Forman, *The Bulldog,* London, 1899, p. 24 and *passim.*
21. Ritvo, *Animal Estate,* pp. 107–13.
22. George Jess, quoted in Ritvo, *Animal Estate,* p. 113.
23. G.M. Trevelyan, *The Seven Years of William IV,* London, 1952, p. 5.
24. *Seven Years of William IV,* p. 5. This, essentially, is the argument of Miles Taylor as well in 'John Bull and the Iconography of Public Opinion in England, c. 1712–1929', *Past and Present,* vol. 13, 1992.
25. *Daily Telegraph,* 13 June 2002.

Acknowledgements

The following historians and scholars offered help and advice: Ronald Hutton, John Brewer, Stella Tillyard, Hugh Cunningham, Andrew Marr, Nicholas Rogers, Richard Humphreys, Tom Jaine, Laura Mason, C. Anne Wilson, Ivan Day, David Eveleigh, Dr Joan Thirsk, Richard Abbott (Birmingham Central Library), Chris Copp, Robert Malcolmson, Alison Locker, Darra Goldstein, Janice Longone, Will Hobson and Xa Sturgis. Su and John Miller in London and Mary Gugenheim and Jon Will in Chicago looked after me and provided places to write. I am extremely indebted to all of them.

Most of my research was done at the British Library. It can't be praised too highly. I am also grateful to the Prints and Drawings Department of the British Museum. Sir John Lucas-Tooth and Mariah Hibbert were kind enough to give me access to and information on the Beefsteak Club. My agent Georgia Garrett read versions and proffered insightful comments and encouragement. Mary Gugenheim kindly checked the proofs.

I would also like to thank the following for permission to use illustrative material: The Bass Museum, Burton upon Trent (7); The Beefsteak Club (11, 12); The Royal Pavilion, Libraries and Museums, Brighton (43); The Bridgeman Art Library (2, 8, 21); Andrew Edmunds, London (36, 42); Ivan Day (46); Iona Antiques, London (48, 50); The Museum of London (4, 6); Tate Britain, London (16); The National Trust (45); the *Sun*, News International, London (1).

Above all, I am grateful to my editor, Jenny Uglow, who worked tirelessly to improve this book. I am embarrassed to think how much I owe her.

Index